Cultural Hybridity and Fixity:

Strategies of Resistance in Migration Literatures

Andrew Nyongesa

Mwanaka Media and Publishing Pvt Ltd,
Chitungwiza Zimbabwe

*

Creativity, Wisdom and Beauty

Publisher:
Mmap
Mwanaka Media and Publishing Pvt Ltd
24 Svosve Road, Zengeza 1
Chitungwiza Zimbabwe
mwanaka@yahoo.com
https//mwanakamediaandpublishing.weebly.com

Distributed in and outside N. America by African Books Collective
orders@africanbookscollective.com
www.africanbookscollective.com

ISBN: 978-0-7974-9547-0
EAN: 9780797495470

© Andrew Nyongesa 2018

All rights reserved.
No part of this book may be reproduced or transmitted in any form or by any means, mechanical or electronic, including photocopying and recording, or be stored in any information storage or retrieval system, without written permission from the publisher

DISCLAIMER
All views expressed in this publication are those of the author and do not necessarily reflect the views of *Mmap*.

ACKNOWLEDGEMENTS

Just as a tomato plant needs a stake so did I need stakes to raise this project to maturation. It gives me particular pleasure to note that most of those mentioned below contributed to the birth and nurture of this project. The evolution of it owes a personal debt to Dr. J.K.S. Makokha of Kenyatta University for his in-depth coverage of African Literature, specifically literatures of Somalia during our course work. His technical advice on topic choice and attention to details cannot be taken for granted.

I want here to acknowledge the foundational advice of Dr. Kimani Kaigai of Kenyatta University, Kericho Campus. Besides being my first supervisor, his insight in postcolonial migration and resourcefulness bolstered my mastery of the topic. It will be absurd to forget his dedication to my work and ability to adhere to deadlines. They are such virtues of work that enabled me to complete this project on time.

Much gratitude to senior lecturers at Kenyatta University: Dr. Paul M. Mukundi, for setting high standards for graduate studies in the Literature Department. His guidance has enabled us to choose quality topics. I also acknowledge Dr. John Mugubi for his guidance on graduate studies and in-depth exposition of Caribbean literature, some of which concerns ambivalence and alienation are similar to those of migration literature. Finally, I recognize Professor Obura, whose wise and fatherly counsel has determined formulation of many careers at the department.

It will be preposterous to forget my colleagues, Julia Njeri Karumba and Asuka Ondigo, for the encouragement and inspiration.

Table of Contents

Abstract..v
Operational Definition of Terms..vi
Chapter 1: Purpose, Scope and Context of the Study.....................1
Chapter 2: Characterization and Author's Concerns.....................40
Chapter 3: Cultural Hybridity and Identity Formation..................84
Chapter 4: Hybridity and Fixity as Modes of Resistance..............126
Chapter 5: Summary and Conclusions..170
Cited Works..176
Appendix 1..185
Appendix 2..187
Appendix 3..189

ABSTRACT

The focus of this project is the examination of identity politics and acts of resistance staged by migrant characters living overseas as represented in Safi Abdi's *Offspring of Paradise (2004)* and *A Mighty Collision of Two Worlds (2002)*. Over the years, literary critics have explored the impact of transnational migrations on identity negotiations of immigrants from Africa and Asia in western cities. However, postcolonial migrant literature from East Africa has received sparse critical attention. This is against the reality that literary works from East Africa, especially from Somalia, profoundly depict the phenomenal postcolonial migration. Using selected strands of postcolonial theory, the study investigates the role of hybridity in textualizing migrant identity formation. The study then evaluates fixity and hybridity as modes of resistance. Finally, the characters are analysed to show how the two modes express concerns typical of migration literature as a genre. The ideas of Stuart Hall, Frantz Fanon, Gayatri Spivak and Homi Bhabha will form a theoretical basis for interpretation. The study is a comprehensive qualitative library research that will proceed via close reading of primary, secondary texts and refereed journal articles.

OPERATIONAL DEFINITION OF TERMS

Binary factions: The phrase is used in the study to mean two distinct, discordant cultures in an eternal state of tension.

Cosmopolitanism: Used in the study to refer to community that has people from diverse backgrounds, races, religions and tribes.

Diaspora: The term has been used in the study to mean a community that has dispersed and settled in a foreign land because of natural disasters, war and other causes in their land.

Essentialism: Used in the study to refer to the belief that some cultures are pure and more important than others are.

Fixed characters: Used in the study to refer to conservative characters that stick to their culture

Fixity: The term is used to refer to the attribute of being proud of one's culture and looking down on the culture of the other group.

Hybridity: It means the migrant adopting accommodating attitude towards the culture of the other group, accepting some of its aspects while holding on one's identity.

Hybrid characters: immigrant characters who opt for hybridity as a coping strategy abroad.

Immigrants: Used in the study to refer to people who arrive in a foreign country from their country voluntarily or involuntarily to live there.

Liminal space: The phrase has been used to refer to the space between two cultures, the border where they negotiate their coexistence (also third space or in-betweenness).

Metropolis: A big city in a former colonizer's territory held by immigrants as a land of opportunities.

Migrancy: Used in this study as synonym for 'migration'.

CHAPTER ONE

Purpose, Scope and Context of the Study

Introduction

The modern world is under constant transition and not even an invention lasts for a year without being replaced. Traditions, customs and beliefs pulsate under the throes of change and no field of knowledge has been left out of this purge as humankind resolves to adopt new lifestyles to better their existence in the world, those that stick to past forms of life become irrelevant; hence to remain relevant, all forms of knowledge adapt to these changes. Literature has not lagged behind, it has adapted to the shift to continue playing its role in the changing, modern society. Unlike the ancient times when movements were tied to droughts and other natural calamities, the contemporary society has many causes of migrations, some of which are voluntarist thereby making the human race more restless. Even those communities that were traditionally perceived as settler communities like Bantus in East Africa are no longer settler; they migrate to other parts of the world to seek for better opportunities. These movements have had a remarkable impact on literature because literature is about people and their experiences in the world. Fatemeh Poujafari and Vahdipour Abdolali write:

> We live in world of constant changes and movements, the result of which nothing is stable and borders have become mixed. The outstanding technological advancements like satellite, internet and modern means of transport and globalization of world

economy are influential factors in making our age the age of mobility and borderlessness. The traditional settler life has given place to a new nomadic lifestyle and migration has become a familiar trend. (679)

The scholars reiterate that the world is today characterized by migrancy, which renders everything temporary and cosmopolitan, by 'everything' we mean, cultural identities, including racial and religious forms of life. They attribute it to the ease with which information and people flow from one part of the world to the other due to revolution in transport and information technology. As humankind changes to adapt to changes brought by migration and globalism, literature has also changed leading to the emergence of a new kind of literature referred to as literature of migration. Sabina Hussain notes that "postcolonial migrant literature comprises of texts by authors with direct or indirect connections to formerly colonized countries" (106). She adds that "these texts not only include first generation authors who live in a former colony but also second generation authors still under the influence of historical and political effects of former colonial times" (106). Vladimir Nabokov, (cited from Jin Ha) observes that "a writer's nationality is of negligible importance; a writer's art is his real passport into foreign lands" (ix). Migrant literature is hence art that traverses boundaries regardless of the author's nationality.

Robin Cohen observes that "transnational migrations are as old as the Jewish dispersal after the destruction of Jerusalem and razing of the walls of the temple by Babylonians in 586 B.C" (2). He refers to it as prototypical, classical victim Diaspora, the only diaspora with capital 'D'. It was then that the word Diaspora was first used. The word is derived from a Greek word "[d]iasperein," which means "dispersal or scattering of seeds" (2). Apart from the Jews, there was forced shipment of at least ten million black people across the Atlantic to offer slave labour. In these mass displacements, subjects were herded to destinations they had not chosen. It was as traumatic as the Jewish experience and Cohen places the African and Jewish Diaspora under one category. He names other types of diaspora: The first type is labour and imperial diaspora, which is diaspora generated by emigration in search for work, to further colonial ambitions or in pursuit of trade. He gives the example of the Turks who entered Europe after the Second World War in search of employment (61). The second type is trade and business diasporas. They are networks of proactive merchants, probably related by blood, that establish commercial interests. For instance, the Indians who benefited from colonial expansion in East Africa. They were permitted by colonial regimes to settle in urban locations such as Nairobi, Kampala and Dar es Salaam.

After the Second World War, migrancy increasingly became more global with people from diverse points of origin, destinations and trajectories than any other epoch of history. Hence forth, there have been flows of migrants, immigrants, guest workers, refugees, asylum seekers and exiles. Stephen Cairns notes that these flows and attempts to settle in foreign lands have been ill-perceived by host countries. Immigrants are viewed as "endangering social cohesion, burdening housing and infrastructure and disrupting the peace of bonafide citizens thereby provoking rejection and discrimination" (2). In some cases, states have enacted laws to deport immigrants to their mother countries. In the year 2000, Immigration and Naturalization Service in United States of America deported 86000 immigrants (Allermann, 4). Migration is fast becoming a contentious issue in the West, where countries have to bear huge finacial burdens to both cater for illegal immigrants and prevent their entry. Some nations had had to go an extra mile into saving those illegal immigrants whose lives are threatened by violent storms at sea. In such cases, adult casualties are treated and deported but underage immigrants are integrated in the western societies.

The end of the Second World War came with independence of colonized nations in Africa and a new form migration emerged. Lau observes that while England's imperial glory was gradually fading in the twentieth century, its capital, London, became a migrant destination (2).There was the *S.S Windrush* generation in 1948, the official arrival of immigrants from West Indies to London. People from Commonwealth nations and Pakistan settled in droves in London in 1950s. Post-colonialism became a reversal of colonialism in that formerly colonized subjects started settling down in imperial capitals like London. In migration literature, expectation is not always commensurate with reality. Moudouma Sydoine notes that the identity of migrants is made complex through their encounter with the unknown. The characters experience feelings of strangeness, otherness, blackness, trauma and feelings of being a refugee (41). Immigrant characters get alienated by the foreignness they experience overseas, the culture shock and discrimination have negative impact on them; consequently, they invent strategies of resistance against discrimination, for instance, hybridity and fixity.

While defining the concept of cultural hybridity, Homi Bhabha gives a hint of what fixity is. He implies that cultural fixity is holding on traditional customs and beliefs as true national culture. In his work, "Commitment to Theory," he observes that fixity not only leads to polarity but also hinders political change. He writes:

> The enunciation of cultural difference problematizes the division of past and present, tradition and modernity and the level of cultural representation. It is the problem of how in signifying the present something comes to be repeated, relocated and translated in the name of tradition, in the guise of a pastness that is not necessarily a faithful sign of historical memory but a strategy of representing authority in terms of the artifice of the archaic. It negates our sense of the origins of the struggle. It questions our sense of cultural synthesis. In the moment of liberatory struggle, Algerian people destroy continuities and constancies of the nationalist tradition, which provided a safeguard against colonial cultural imposition. They are now free to negotiate and translate their cultural identities. The native intellectual who identifies the people with true national culture will be disappointed. (9-23)

Bhabha, in this passage avers that cultural fixity is not necessarily a reminder of our history but a symbol of the obsolete traditions. It undermines our struggle for freedom and peaceful coexistence. Citing the example of Algeria, he suggests that the fight for independence was a fight against both colonialism and cultural fixity, "[c]ontinuities and constancies of the national tradition," (208). With independence, the natives are now free to establish a new identity by hybridity. He therefore exalts hybridity as the space between the culture of the immigrant and the culture of the dominant group. The character loves his culture but is also open to aspects of the foreign culture. As he negotiates with the dominant group, he "destroys the mirror of representation in which cultural knowledge is continuously revealed as an expanding code," (208). For him, hybridity is an effective strategy of resistance.

William Safran notes that diaspora has been stretched to cover almost any ethnic or religious minority that is dispersed physically from its original homeland regardless of whether physical, cultural or emotional links exist between the community and the home country. He defines diaspora as expatriate minority communities that share a number of features: First, they or their ancestors have been dispersed from specific original centre to two or more foreign regions. Secondly, they retain a collective memory vision or myth about their original homeland. Thirdly, they believe they are not and cannot be fully accepted by their host society, hence feel partly alienated from it. Fourthly, they regard their ancestral homeland as their true or ideal home. Furthermore, they believe they should collectively be committed to restoration of their original homeland to its safety and prosperity (83-84). Diaspora has experienced several applications henceforth. Rainer Baubock and Thomas Faist single out three features of contemporary definitions of diaspora. The first relates to causes of migration. Older notions refer to forced dispersal like the Jewish example but recent notions refer to any kind including trade diasporas (12). The second characteristic links experiences abroad and the motherland. Older notions like Safran's imply a return to a homeland but newer notions encourage continuous linkages across borders. The third characteristic concerns integration of immigrants and minorities into host countries. Older notions hold that immigrants do not fully integrate in host communities (13). Newer notions emphasize cultural hybridity. These were postulated by Homi Bhabha and Stuart Hall.

Cohen, a proponent of the newer notions of diaspora, singles out repetition in Safran's features given that four features are related to homeland. He adds four other features about evolution and character of diasporic groups (6-29). First, "[t]he inclusion in diaspora, groups that disperse for colonial and voluntarist reasons; second, there should be recognition of positive virtues of retaining diasporic identity than that implied in Safran's list. The tension between an ethnic, national and transnational identity is a creative, enriching one because anxiety in diaspora motivates achievement," (7). Thirdly, diasporas mobilize collective identity, not just in a place of settlement but also in solidarity with co-ethnic members of other countries; bonds among them are more intimate than those among citizens. Abdi's characters portray most of these features.

Safi Abdi was born and raised in Somalia until the age of thirteen. She is one of the children in a family of nine. Her father was killed during the Somalia civil war in the early nineties. Compelled by insecurity at home, she migrated to Dubai where she lives to the present. She is a holder of a degree in English and Literature and diploma in creative writing from the institute of Children's Literature, West Redding, Connecticut, United States of America. Published in 2002, *A Mighty Collision of Two Worlds* was her first novel. The novel explores experiences of Somali diaspora in the United States of America driven there by the search for better education and economic opportunities. Anisa, the heroine of the novel, goes to Fairwood School in United States on a school exchange program and takes advantage to have college education. Under the influence of Western culture, she gets married to a white atheist and her struggle for identity commences. Abdi's treatment of migration themes distinguishes her as a migrant writer. It is not surprising that she pursued her further studies in the United States of America. In 2004, Abdi published *Offspring of Paradise,* the tale of the harrowing experience of the civil war in Somalia and the plight of refugees who migrate to western cities for refuge. Abdi draws heavily from her experience both as a transnational immigrant and a refugee to depict issues of migration in her novels. Although her works have not won any prizes, her writing has a future on the corpus of migrant literature. She is now a freelance writer, a homemaker and mother of three children. This project focuses on narratives about diasporic peoples from East Africa, with a particular emphasis on Somalia diaspora.

A Historical Background to Somali Migration

The Somali have been victims of xenophobia around the world, the worst being in the worst being in Cape Town, in September 2006 when thirty one Somalis were killed. Questions have been raised to find out why millions of Somalians migrate from Somalia to foreign lands. Press releases about illegal immigrants of Somali origin perishing in the Mediterranean Sea, on the way to Italy as recent as April 2015 are astounding. Historical sources name a number of causes of migration. To begin with, historians refer to political violence as the major cause of migration of the Somali from Somalia to other nations. Robert Hess points out the root cause of political strife as Somalia's Italian colonial heritage beginning with the occupation that took longer than other African nations. Whereas British colonial conquest in Kenya ended in 1905 with the conquest of the Nandi under Koitalel Arap Samoei, Italy effected Somalia occupation as late as 1927 (152). Under strict directives by the fascist Prime Minister, Benito Mussolini, the Somalia Governor; De Vecchi carried out the conquest with a brutality that left severe scars on the Somali populace. The commissioner at Obbla, a Fascist colonel, would brood no insubordination on the part of the Somali sultan, effecting the occupation with such brutality that left indelible wounds on the Somali community; apparently, the political violence is mimicry of the colonial master.

Moreover, there was little or no education for the masses during the colonial period. Historians agree that unlike other East African nations where western education was emphasized, the British and Italians scarcely influenced nomadic tribes of Somalia in education matters. Robert observes that no attempt was made to Italianize the Somali throughout most of the colonial period (169). Conflict between the Catholic Church and fascist government in Italy was the root cause of this failure. Illiteracy meant that the Somali continued to exist in their sectarian groupings for a long time. Secondly, poor governance is the other cause of political strife in Somalia. Given a colonial heritage of violence, division and illiteracy, the post independence government could not last. Saadia Tooval observes that different economic, political and administrative patterns had developed between the north and the south yet a successful union required that the two territories became more closely integrated in these respects (50). Furthermore, the new political system that colonial masters had forged was ill adapted to the traditional political organization of Somali people. With little western education, Somalis were comfortable with their clan based political system. The new 'borrowed' political system could not work (Gundel, 257). With the burden of poor governance, relegated Somali clans like the Isaaq migrated abroad in the sixties as they had lost their assets and were denied access to new resources. From 1973, Somalia became a major labour exporter to oil producing Arab countries. Up to two hundred thousand people migrated this way, over half from the Isaaq clan (Gundel, 263). This marked the beginning of mass migration of Somalians from their nation after independence, millions thronged overseas in search for peace and opportunities.

Another cause of migration from Somalia is insufficient natural resources and poor agricultural potential. Robert notes that right from the colonial period, Somalia was not agriculturally endowed. Attempts by the Italian governor to entice investors with agricultural concessions in 1910 met with scant success. Seven out of eleven concessions were abandoned (111). The Agronomist Romolo Onor, who was invited to research on the agricultural potential of Somalia, got gravely depressed and committed suicide in 1918 (114). In her historical novel *Black Mamba Boy,* Nadifa Mohamed presents migrant characters who say they are migrating because their country has nothing, "[e]verywhere I go, I meet Somalis, always from the north standing at the crossroads looking up at the sky. They all say the same thing, "[t]here is nothing in my country, I will go back when I can afford some camels," (274). Most characters in Mohamed's *Black Mamba Boy* migrate from Somalia to Sudan, Egypt, Palestine and to Britain in search for means of livelihood. Jama Gure, the central character traverses all these regions because of the poverty of his situation, he ends up in the Italian army to fight the Allies during the Second World War.

Somalia has the longest coastline in East Africa, along the Indian Ocean. Proximity to the ocean with a long history of migration and trade has made them vulnerable to migrancy. Anne Bang in her book *Sufis and Scholars of the Sea, Family Networks in East Africa,* notes that the Indian Ocean was an established arena of migration, "[p]eople moved over the sea, in a crisscrossing pattern, governed by winds," (ix). They traveled with goods, ideas and many other things. Somalis learnt the culture of migration by sea from Arabs, to trade and spread Islam.

To sum up, migration of Somalians therefore comes under a wide range of diaspora. It is victim diaspora because the immigrants are forced by political strife to seek refuge in foreign countries, as is the case in Abdi's *Offspring of Paradise*. The Somali state has not succeeded in unifying national identity of different clans around one leader. It is labour diaspora because characters migrate in search for better education and means of livelihood in Western cities as is the case in Abdi's *A Mighty Collision of Two Worlds*.

1.1 STATEMENT OF THE PROBLEM

In recent years, a number of literary studies have analysed Asian and African migration to Western cities. Sydoine Moudouma Moudouma in his thesis investigates the way migrations affect identity formations using literary works from Central and West Africa. In spite of this effort, there are very few studies at the nexus of postcolonial migration and identity politics with reference to East African literary writers. This is in spite of availability of migrant literature, especially in Somalia after the fall of Siad Barre in 1991. These writers have not only delved into literature of migration as a nascent genre but depicted its characteristic themes. The heroes and heroines respond by cultural hybridity and cultural fixity in the face of discrimination in diaspora. This study examines identity politics and acts of resistance staged by migrant characters living abroad. Using selected strands of postcolonial theory, the study investigates the role of hybridity in textualising migrant identity formation. The study then evaluates fixity and hybridity as modes of resistance. Finally, the characters are analysed to show how the two modes depict concerns typical of migration literature as a genre.

1.2 RESEARCH OBJECTIVES

This study is guided by three objectives, namely, to:
i) Discuss the role of characters on the central concerns of the novelist.
ii) Examine the role of hybridity in formation of diasporic identity.
iii) Compare and contrast fixity and hybridity as modes of resistance against the dominant group.

1.3 RESEARCH QUESTIONS

i) How does the novelist textualise her concerns at the level of characterization?
ii) How does hybridity affect the identity of migrant characters?
iii) Is fixity better than hybridity as a mode of resistance in diaspora?

1.3 RESEARCH ASSUMPTIONS

i) The novelist effectively uses characterization to textualise her concerns.
ii) Hybridity plays a significant role in formation of diasporic identity
iii) Hybridity is a better form of resistance than fixity as it eludes the politics of polarity.

1.5 JUSTIFICATION OF THE STUDY

There are many postcolonial studies on the literature of migration in Africa and beyond. Most of these studies have clearly expounded on the efforts of immigrants to negotiate their way at the heart of discrimination and oppression to form their own identity as people. Some characters choose the path of fixity by sticking to their culture while others choose the path of hybridity by mimicking the oppressor to negotiate and destroy hegemonic prejudice. Literary scholars have carried out studies on African immigrant characters under racist repressions overseas but there is sparse critical attention in postcolonial migration on the Somali, Muslim immigrants from East Africa in western cities. This is so in spite of the millions of Somali, Muslim immigrants who strive to survive against discrimination in Christian and secular majority in western cities. Whereas focus on Somali writers often stops with Nuruddin Farah, recent times have produced other writers such as Nadifa Mohamed, Safi Abdi, Waris Diriye, Abdirazack Yusuf Osman among others. It is the contention of this study that criticism on other writers from Somalia like Safi Abdi is important. Her two novels have not been subjected to any known study yet they are rich in postcolonial migration and strategies of resistance.

1.6 THE SCOPE AND DELIMITATION OF THE STUDY

The study will limit itself to the two novels of Abdi. They shall form a basis for analysis of migrant characters and fixity and hybridity as strategies of resistance to the dominant group in diaspora. The texts are *A Mighty Collision of Two Worlds (2002)* and *Offspring of Paradise (2004)*.

1.7 LITERATURE REVIEW

1.71 Introduction

The literature review begins with a discussion of those studies that are concerned with strategies of textual resistance by migrant characters and then shift focus to those that examine themes typical of migration literature as a genre. Given that Abdi is a debut novelist, there is no relevant literature on her works.

1.72 Literature on Strategies of Resistance

Walter Roland looks at the way identity is formed in a cosmopolitan world. He notes that in, "[a] world characterized by disjunctive flows of objects with people from different places, origins and diversity, cultures of people are affected by global elements through mutual exchanges or borrowing,"(118). In the contemporary world in which cultural diversity is magnified on one hand and cultural hybridization mounting on the other, it compels scholars to reconsider cultural identity relations. He observes that albeit cultural identity is determined by one's ethnic group and tribe, it fixes identity just temporarily. Because of the interaction between past traditions and emerging values, the immigrant constantly recreates his identity. His identity is incessantly remade: "[c]onstantly in a process of being and becoming" (118). The identity of the immigrant and racially oppressed person is formed out of his difference from the dominant group (118). The author sums up that to have an identity is to be located in the third space where we respect the Other's differences. That cultural fixity prevents benevolent interactions among people (121).

Although the study is based on James Clifford's theoretical argument, it is very enriching to this study. There are parallels between Clifford's argument and Bhabha's concept of hybridity, which is the interpretive grid of this study. Walter Roland's "shifting open site" refers to is Bhabhan 'third space' from which the immigrant shares his or her experiences to coexist, on one hand and threaten the dominant group on the other. Whereas subalternisation in the metropolis in Walter Roland's study is based on race, this study is based on both religion and race.

Martin Genetsch in his thesis, "Difference and Identity in Contemporary Anglo-Canadian Fiction," observes that colonialism and neocolonialism compelled people to migrate to different parts of the world. As much as millions of people from Caribbean, Africa and Asia migrated to England and America and altered the composition of the West, the changes have created unique cultural identities. Genetsch stresses that migration has great impact on both the host society and the migrant himself. He adds that the greatest challenge for those leaving their ancestral homes is the construction of a new identity (4). The migrant is concerned with making life in diaspora livable by either trying to relive the old culture or adopting the new altogether. The author notes that identities are constructed in a principle open to change thereby emphasizing cultural difference should not be the major characteristic of migration literature. This study builds on Genetsch's study because he expounds on cultural hybridity and fixity. In his view, identity can only be constructed where there is 'openness to change'. The cultural difference he insists, should not be a prime feature of migration literature, is cultural fixity and 'the principle open to change' is hybridity. His emphasis on identity changing potential of migration is relevant to this study, which looks at the impact of hybridity on diasporic identity.

Rebecca Malcom looks at the way migrants respond to names imposed on them by the dominant group. She interviews six global immigrants and analyses their art to determine how they cope with imposed identities. Through their works, they focus on assimilation, statelessness and othering hence challenging cultural fixity. They combine diverse cultures creating transnational spaces that challenge nation state system. She observes that art by people of diverse backgrounds creates captivating fusions that permit commentary on multiple cultures. She gives the example of Joseph Beuys' "Coyote, I like America and America likes(?) me." The Coyote symbolizes the native American people and their culture, which is being threatened with annihilation by capitalist materialism. Here is a fusion of native American concepts with colonial America collective identity (19). She asserts that artists, Sherrier Levine and Henny Holzer use photography and text to express diverse identities that challenge dominant groups. This study builds on Malcom's study because the combination of diverse cultures to create transnational spaces is a reference to hybridity, which is a strategy of textual resistance against the dominant group. Malcom asserts that it challenges the nation state system, in other words, it contests essentialist views. Although Malcom's study seeks data from both literary and picture drawing artists, this study will focus on literary artists only.

Esther Hor Ying Lau in her thesis depicts South Asian immigrants and their identity conflicts as presented in contemporary British novels. In the first chapter, she discusses the identity politics of postcolonial subjects in Zadie Smith's *White Teeth* with Homi Bhabha's hybridity as a theoretical framework. The study examines different levels of hybridity and identities in processes that are formulated via assimilation, integration and resistance. Instead of nostalgia, second generation migrants embrace their hybridity better than their parents because they are hybridized and have defied fixity; thereby more open to new values. In the second chapter, Lau distinguishes the migrant from the hybrid. That the migrant is the character who arrives in the adopted country with a baggage, which prevents him from fully integrating into adopted country. The hybrid is born in the adopted country and does not miss the mother land; however, both are racially discriminated and are under orientalist scrutiny(25). Lau's study also looks at the role of religion in formation of diasporic identity. Some characters in Hanif Kureish's novel, *The Black Album* turn to Islamic fundamentalism as a form of identity. This study is similar to Lau's study in that they both examine the role of hybridity as a strategy of textual resistance by immigrants in the face of discrimination overseas. Religion also plays an important role in augmenting cultural difference in this study; the immigrants are Muslims but the host country has Christians and atheists. Nevertheless, Lau's study differs with this study slightly when it limits hybridity to intermarriage. This study looks at hybridity as an attitude that anyone can nurture, any person can acquire to learn and accept people of other religions, tribes and races as they are. In this study, a hybrid is neither a mulatto nor an alienated person; a hybrid is one who recognizes his or her culture but is willing to appreciate other people's culture and coexist with them. Mixed marriage is just a metaphor of hybridity.

Bahmanpour Bahareh in her thesis focuses on identity crises of discriminated diasporic women as depicted by Jhumpa Lahiri in three stories in *Interpreter of Maladies*. The study looks at *Interpreter of Maladies* as an anthology concerned with Indian Americans whose migration has compelled to be caught between the Indian traditions and a totally different western world, which has resulted in an ongoing struggle to adjust between two worlds. The study, which draws on the ideas of Homi Bhabha and Gayatri Chakravorty Spivak observes that by allowing the marginalized females to be voiced, Lahiri's stories prepare a space through which the oppressed can speak (43). Bahmanpour cites the story, "This Blessed House," where hybridity is expressed in the character of Twinkle whose assimilation leaves little room for biased cultural orientation. She has accepted the culture of the Other in that she has taken an Irish poet for her masters thesis. When she finds the statue of Christ, she says, "[w]e are good little Hindus," but leaves a kiss on top of Christ's head. When the white guests consider her name as weird, she shows no shame and sorrow. The study holds that this dynamic positive hybridity in Twinkle makes her survival definite and gives her superiority over other female characters. Twinkle's degree of hybridity needs enough exposure to the culture of the Other to develop to the hybrid space.

This study builds on Bahmnapour's study in that it elevates hybridity as a strategy of resistance. Twinkle has learnt to survive in the face of discrimination. Secondly, the study does not equate hybridity to mixed marriage. Twinkle is not married to a white American but has accepted some western values. She has taken an Irish poet for her thesis and is not affected when they throw vibes at her funny name. Even if Hana in *Offspring of Paradise* is not married to a white man she is a hybrid in the sense that she dresses like the whites, keeps a Christian friend, Helen and has had western education. With more exposure to western culture, she will develop to the hybrid space.

Idil Bozkurt, in his thesis, *Migration and Hybridity: Stereoscopic Vision in the Novels of Rushdie, Mukherjee and Gosh* analyses three Indian-English writers who examine challenges and aspirations of migrant characters by presenting characters that undergo transformation in their identity as a result of migration. The thesis is founded on the premise that diversity in the immigrant gives her diverse identities that negotiate with diverse cultures. The study adds that hybridity, which represents diverse cultural identities provides ground for creativity and resistance to prejudices against the dominant group. He notes that Salman Rushdie proposes hybridity as a strategy of resistance for despised immigrants and racially discriminated groups. Giving the example of Mukherjee Bharatis *Jasmine*, he observes that travel gives women immigrants a variety of subject positions that bolster resistance against subjugation. The study concludes that socio-cultural spaces like migrant identities are hybrid realms in which the lines between Self and the Other, here and there, are blurred. The presence of migrant characters in the novels forces metropolis to not only encounter Otherness but also discover the other within, which gives way to tolerance. Bozkurt's study is beneficial to this study because it proposes hybridity as a mode of resistance by immigrants to discrimination in diaspora. It aptly places the migrant characters in the field of postcolonial studies. However, it differs with this study as it absolutely ignores fixity as an alternative strategy of textual resistance.

Referring to Caribbean literature as polyrhythmic performance, Marie France Faulkner examines the claim that in a world that is in a state of constant fluctuation, Caribbean literary writers offer a singular perspective of negotiating identity away from binary forms of the centre and the margin (2). She adds that the writers offer a fresh and transnational vision of the self. The study refers to the mixing of discourses in Caribbean works as a liberating, dynamic force that creates new subject positions to develop along lines of likeness and variance. She notes that at a time when matters of identity are controversial, the celebration of cosmopolitanism, fluidity and ambivalence offers new ways of eluding essentialist forms. This study builds on Faulkher's study because both studies refer to hybridity as a mode of eluding the politics of polarity. The mixing of discourses is a reference to the third space where immigrant characters adopt aspects of the dominant group and adulterate claims to racial purity.

Paul Maina Mukundi investigates postcolonial fiction writers that have viewed cultural experiences of African, Indian and Caribbean people after colonization. The study examines the colonialist's attempts to impose hybridity on subjects with the aim of substituting indigenous languages and religion. Using the works of Ngugi Wa Thiong'o and Zake Mda from Africa, Mahasweta Devi's and Arudhati Roy's from India and Jamaica Kincald's and Maryse Condes from Caribbean,

Mukundi shows how these communities are changed by externally imposed colonial systems. Mukundi's study is similar to this study because it shows the potential of hybridity to infiltrate and destroy another culture. Nonetheless it differs from this study because it dwells on forced hybridity initiated by the dominant group to annihilate cultural attributes of the marginalized group. This study is concerned with voluntary hybridity in which immigrant characters willingly enter the third space to erode the attributes of the majority.

Moudouma observes that there is a relationship between identity formation and migration of characters from one country to another. Whether by one's volition or compulsion, the process of migration from one's motherland to a foreign nation changes the migrant who is compelled to negotiate with new cultures and tensions always mount as he confronts strange cultures of the host society. He adds that the entrapment in distinct selves confers upon them a double identity (4). Analysing literary works of African writers like Abdulrazak Gurnah, Brian Chikwava, Jude Dibia, Buchi Emecheta, Marie Beatrice Umutesi, Phaswane Mpe, Simao Kikamba, Alex Agyei Agyiri and Binyavanga Wainaina, Moudouma observes that Africanity in African immigrants is more significant after they leave Africa (7). He cites Frantz Fanon's *Black Skin White Masks* to show how Africans are mistreated overseas (33). Relegation by the dominant group compels African immigrants in diaspora to embrace their Africanity; consequently the Zulu from South Africa, Igbo of Nigeria and Kikuyus of Kenya view themselves, first as Africans. This study builds on Moudouma's study because it is concerned with immigrants' identity formation in the face of dominant group in diaspora. 'The 'entrapment in distinct selves' is reference to hybridity that migrant characters adopt to collaborate and contest the foreign culture. The determination to nurture Africanity to resist discrimination is what is hereby referred to as cultural fixity. Hana, in *Offspring of Paradise*, cultivates high sense of nationalism when she realizes that her people are denigrated and relegated.

1.73 Literature on Themes of Migration Literature

Aalstad Gregersen is concerned with identity changes of migrant characters in David Malouf's *Remembering Babylon*. He observes that the description of landscape as it changes in the novel visualizes the character's identity changes towards a new identity. As time elapses, migrant characters start to acknowledge that they are crossbreeds and hybrid identities (30). By focusing on different aspects of the novel, Gregersen discusses identity, hybridity, ambivalence, displacement and othering. By investigating Malouf's vivid descriptions, the author explores different facets of identity at the meeting point of two opposing cultures: British and aborigines. The issues that emerge as the central characters change into a hybrid identity are considered too. This study builds on Gregersen's study because it investigates the manner in which migrant characters build identities by hybridity in diaspora. Like the above study, it also explores ambivalence, hybridity and other themes typical of migration literature.

Luca Elena is concerned with literary depiction of cultural identity formation in the works of German-Romanian authors, Richard Wagner and Hertha Mueller. The writers question the tribe as a basis of nationalism and interrogate conservative definitions of Germanness based on biological and state centered parameters. Studying Wagner's fiction, Holden examines the way he constructs cultural identities and reinvents himself as a writer during Ceausescu's autocratic regime and after immigration to West Germany. Luca analyses the way Wagner's characters negotiate identity between the periphery in Romania and the Centre in West Germany, which combine Romanian and German languages. The identity of Mueller's prime movers is characterized by alienation as a result of trauma in Banat-Swabian village and communist Romania. This study builds on Luca's study pertaining identity formation among immigrants. Just as Richard Wagner's characters negotiate for identity in Romania, so does this study look at the way Abdi's protagonists negotiate for identity in Western cities. The combination of Romanian and German languages is a reference to hybridity, which Anisa turns to in Abdi's *A Mighty Collision of Two Worlds*. Mueller's depiction of alienation is relevant to this study as it analyses themes typical of migration literature. Anisa Haji for instance suffers internal fragmentation in *A Mighty Collision of Two Worlds*.

Dieter Wilde notes that the novelist Hanif Kureishi's uses Bhabha's third space to show how different identities within one person surrender to one another in the *Buddha of Suburbia*. He observes that the novel is an exposition of humankind's hybrid nature given that the protagonist, Karim, is a mulatto (of white mother and Pakistani father) living in a London Suburb. The identity impasse he faces could be anybody's, especially the immigrant's. He notes that Karim is a 'qualified Englishman' but with a feeling of both Englishness and Indiannness. He writes, "[t]he East exists as an underground presence within western identity" (7). This study builds on Wilde's study because Karim's mixed decent metaphorically signifies hybridity, which is prime concern in migration literature. The here and there feeling he experiences depicts ambivalence, which is typical of migration literature. Nevertheless, it slightly differs with this study in terms of sex and sexuality.

Moira Luraschi looks at postcolonial literature in Italy. In the study, she asserts that most of these postcolonial writers are women from Somalia, Ethiopia and Eritrea who left the Horn of Africa as refugees fleeing autocratic regimes. In the study, she observes that migration is a prospect to revise the past and embrace mixed culture (10). She studies the novelist Igiaba Scego, a writer of Somali descent who delves deeply into the theme of double identity. Scego was born in Italy; her parents left Somalia after Siad Barre's coup in 1969. She is an Italian citizen and lives in Rome. In her first novel, *Rhoda,* the main character is caught between two cultures: Italian and Somali. She is in opposition to her aunt Barni who is still linked to Somalia and to her sister Aisha who loves Italian culture. Rhoda becomes a prostitute and when she discovers that she is HIV positive, she returns to Somalia and is killed while resisting a rape attempt. Rhoda's body has scars of a cultural encounter: violated by Italian clients and killed by Somali people. The study compares Rhoda to Ali Farah's Cristina Ubi in *Domenica Axad* who is caught in between the separation of her Somali father from her Italian mother. The study sums up that the migrant writer in Italy enjoys a double point of view and avoids cultural fixity. They have shown how the immigrant is part of the dominant group and how identities are built and negotiated. Luraschi's study is invaluable to this study since it is relevant to our area of study; Scego's parents hail from Somalia like Abdi. They migrate from Somalia due to reasons similar to Abdi's: Political strife. The study examines double identity or hybridity, a major concern of migration literature. This study will examine characteristic themes of migration literature in Abdi's fiction.

Chad Montouri analyses the works of African writers: Donato Ndongo, Maximiliano Nkogo, Najat El Hachmi and Tahar Ben Jelloun to demonstrate how gender and migration interact to destroy any fixed ideas of the migration experience in Africa. Albeit the authors depict migrant characters from Senegal, Cameroon, Equitorial Guinea and Morocco, they all go to Spain. Montuori notes that the migratory journey from Africa to Spain is a space where norms of gender and sexuality are questioned. The study is based on the post-colonial theory's tenet that changes in identity occur because of migration. The writers chosen in the study reject a notion of stable identity (5). Citing Stuart Hall, the study observes that the act of migration forces the protagonist to resolve many internal battles over the past and the present. The movement compels him to develop a double consciousness towards home and host communities hence becoming the embodiment of modernity. As he negotiates with the new changes, his identity is inevitably changed (6). This study builds on Montouri's study since it looks at how identity is formed by migration of characters to foreign lands. The 'development of double conciousness' is indirect reference to ambivalence, one of the themes of migration literature, a concern of this study. Nonetheless, this study does not concern itself with the relationship between gender and migration.

1.74 Conclusion

There is no doubt that migrant characters adopt cultural fixity and cultural hybridity as strategies of textual resistance against discrimination in migration literature. Although the latter is similar to any other form of literature, it expresses certain ideas, for instance hybridity, ambivalence, alienation and abandonment and return, which make it singular.

1.8 THEORETICAL FRAMEWORK

The interpretive grid of this study is the post-colonial theory. Bill Ashcroft and his colleagues observe that "it is a theory that studies the cultural, intellectual realities and tensions that occurred in many nations from the beginning of colonial contact" (1). It emerged when the colonized started to reflect and express tension which followed after disruption by the mixture of imperial culture and native ways.

Post-colonialism and its prominent theorists have contributed to migration literature by identifying a framework of features and principles. Poujafari Fatemeh and Vahidpour Abdolali observe that the primary focus of this literature on marginal groups brings it under postcolonial theory. Post-colonialism in its most recent definition is concerned with persons from groups outside the dominant groups and therefore places subaltern groups in a position to subvert the authority of those with hegemonic power (686). Bill Ashcroft notes that post-colonial theory entails migration, slavery, suppression, resistance, representation and influences to discourses to imperial Europe (2). The theory can be applied to the topic of migration because migrants are positioned at the margins of society and are subject to discrimination of the majority. Taking into account the fact that post-colonial studies turn the world upside down, a study that looks at issues from the view of the despised immigrant aptly comes under it (Young, 2). Post-colonialism explores all ambiguities and complexities of diverse cultural experiences. Ashcroft expounds that the hyphen in the term stands for material effects of colonization, the enormous diversities and the hidden responses to it throughout the world (3). The crucial concepts of post colonialism are as follows:

1.81 Orientalism
The Creation of Binary Opposition

In his work, *Orientalism,* Edward Said observes that European orientalist scholars divided the world by creation of two binary factions: the occident and the orient. That the occident is the West and comprises of the Europeans and the orient is the East, comprising of Arabs, Chinese and Japanese.

Skewed Definition
Orientalist scholars, according to Said, construct the factions as different within the perimeter of their knowledge. They create the West and East as fixed unequal blocs. They construct the West as strong, rational, humane and powerful as opposed to the East that is weak, cruel, irrational and sexually unstable. He writes:

> Europe is powerful and articulate. Asia is defeated and distant. It is Europe that articulates the orient, this articulation is a prerogative not of puppet master, but of a genuine creator whose life giving power represents the otherwise silent and dangerous space beyond familiar boundaries. The orient insinuates danger. Rationality is undermined by Eastern excesses. (57)

Expounding Said's ideas, Yegenoglu Meyda observes that by using diverse works from literary, scientific and historical disciplines, orientalist scholars draw a distinction between the West and the East, of which knowledge they used to subjugate the East (17).

Orientalism is invaluabe to this study because by creation of West/East, strong/weak, superior/inferior, civilized/backward; chaste/sensual, rational/sentimental factions, orientalist scholars posited a polarity or duality that is typical of cultural fixity, a strategy of textual resistance in this study. Orientalism is an essentializing discourse same as immigrant/dominant group situation we find in Abdi's novels. Said implies that the two factions, created by orientalists are static and distinct hence in an eternal state of tension devoid of any prospect of peace. The immigrants, viewed as inferior and 'backward', seclude themselves from the dominant group that drool in a false image of superiority, strength and rationality thereby polarizing the host nation.

1.82 Representation

Gayatri Charkravorty Spivak questions the notion of representation in postcolonial studies. Poststructuralists crown the intellectual as a transparent medium through which the voices of the oppressed can be represented (67-72). Spivak contends that the colonized subaltern subject is irretrievably heterogeneous. She asks, "[c]an this difference be articulated? And if so by whom?" (79-80). In other words, to what extent does Abdi represent the heterogeneous Somali immigrants in western cities. There are those who adore their traditions and those who detest them. There are those in the third space. For Spivak, Abdi may either misrepresent them or in the attempt to give them voice start silencing them. An attempt to give the patriots a voice will silence the hybrids. Spivak gives the British example who in attempt to speak for oppressed widows by banning Sati ended up silencing the Hindu culture. Can Abdi avoid this? Is representation plausible? Apparently, the subaltern cannot speak; therefore the intellectual remains a medium. The study will apply Spivak's notion of representation to interrogate Abdi's concerns to determine her effectiveness.

1.83 Nationalism

Colonialism Destroys National culture
Frantz Fanon, in *The Wretched of the Earth,* looks at national culture in new independent nations. He observes that colonialism, steeped in prejudices, erodes national culture after centuries of colonial exploitation. It becomes a conglomeration of behavioural patterns and creativity and passion are eradicated (172).

Creation of National Culture
The leaders of independent nations should embark on creation of national culture. Fanon defines national culture as all efforts made by people to describe and improve their situation via thoughtful selection of practices that will bolster their existence (168). During the formation of national culture the new leaders should work in step with the people to shape the future. They should not reject those new practices and customs that the people have opted for.

National Culture is not African Culture
Fanon emphasizes that in their efforts to create national culture, revolutionaries and native intellectuals should not relive precolonial past. National culture does not mean a return to precolonial traditions and so leaders should not concentrate efforts on resuscitating traditions to erect a tradition similar to negritude with a delusion to dicover a people's aspirations. He writes, "[n]ational culture is no folklore where an abstract populism is convinced it has uncovered the popular truth. It is not some congealed mass of noble gestures, in other words less and less connected with the reality of the people," (168).

Fanon's concept of nationalism is beneficial to this study since it expounds on cultural fixity and hybridity, which are strategies of resistance in this study. That the creation of national culture should not be a license to embrace cultural fixity. His refusal to return to precolonial traditions is a warning against cultural fixity which will proceed contrary to the people's wishes. That the people, who have fought for liberation, have created a new platform to create a national culture and so the leaders should be careful to work "in step with the people," (168). At this point, Fanon refers to cultural hybridity since the people desire to adopt that which is good from the modern ways of life. He asserts that African leaders that are still striving for African culture will do no more than compare coins and sarcophagi. Fanon lays the foundation of cultural hybridity.

1.84 Cultural Identity

Gayatri Spivak, one of the indomitable voices in postcolonial studies, deconstructs poststructuralist claims that human individuals have no control over their identity. Michael Foucault and Gilles Deluze, proponents of the theory assert that we are not authors of ourselves. We do not construct our identities, we have it written for us. That the subject cannot be sovereign over construction of selfhood. That our identities are constructed from positions outside ourselves. In her essay "Can the Subaltern Speak?" she is surprised because when the two scholars talk about the oppressed groups and workers, (subalterns in her view) they empower them to construct their identity (67-72). They talk of the working class as sovereign subjects and restore to them a fully centred conciousness. Spivak implies that the individual can therefore construct their identities. Postcolonial scholars agree on two facets that determine cultural identity: Fixity and hybridity.

1.85 Cultural Fixity

In his work, "Cultural identity and Diaspora," Stuart Hall comes up with models of cultural identity that define transition of identity of the Caribbean populace. First, he postulates the traditional model that views identity in terms of one shared culture, hiding inside the many. Hall refers to it as artificial for cultural values are imposed on people because they share a history and ancestry. Citing the Caribbean example, Hall asserts that Caribbeans use this model to seek rediscovery of identity in Africa given their African origin (393). He likens this to what Frantz Fanon calls "passionate research," (393). Hall points out that such identity was crucial in postcolonial struggles but is not relevant in the contemporary, cosmopolitan world.

In his work "Comitment to Theory," Bhabha expounds on the concept of cultural fixity. He observes that fixity is a barrier to positive change. Referring to Fanon, he stresses that perpetual insistence on past traditions hinders transformation. He asserts that Fanon's metaphor that the people are in "[f]luctuating movement of occult instability," is not plausible without acknowledging the third space (9-23). The 'flactuating movement' for Bhabha refers to the peoples desire to hybridize the values with emerging changes in science and technology, which will remain a mirage if they choose the path of cultural fixity. The leaders of the independence movements are the torch bearers of hybridity where they spearhead cultural exchanges and transformation of people into mutants. At the third space, Bhabha holds that there is no stagnation. He gives the example of Algeria, a people's traditions only protected them against colonialism. After the struggle for independence, they are free to establish a new national culture by hybridisation. Those native intellectuals who want to return the people to precolonial traditions should brace for disappointment because during the struggle Algerians,"[d]estroyed continuities and constancies of the nationalist tradition. They are now free to negotiate and translate their national identities," (9-23). Cultural fixity is central to this study as it is a strategy of resistance. Hall implies that it is a resistance strategy owing to its vital role in postcolonial struggles.

1.86 Cultural Hybridity

Stuart Hall postulates a contemporary model of cultural identity. It is the model not based on Fanon's rediscovery of identity but the 'production of identity' (Hall, 393). He contends that cultural identity is a process that keeps changing from state to state and given that history intervened through slavery and colonialism, Caribbeans should ask themselves what they have become, instead of who they were. He defines cultural identities as "temporary forms of identification within dialogues of history and culture" (394). Therefore one needs not fix himself on a certain foundation of culture. He writes, "[c]ultural identity is not a fixed essence at all lying unchanged outside history and culture... it is not once-and for-all. It is not a fixed origin on which we can make some final and absolute Return", (395). Hall questions Edward Brathwaite's yearning to recover a lost Africa because with the fluid nature of cultural identity, the original Africa is no longer there. To imagine that Africa is same is colluding with the West in the delusion that Africa is a timeless zone of primitive and unchanging past (399). Bhabha expounds on Fanon's and Hall's ideas. He notes that

Fanon's 'struggle in step with the people' is a desire to enter the third space where the native culture and the colonizer's culture negotiate and yield a hybrid. He defines and clarifies the concept of hybridity- the space between the colonizer and the colonized, with attributes of the two essentialist groups, which challenges the claims to superiority. Although the term hybridity refers to mixture of races or miscegenation, Bhabha's sense of mixture evoked by the word is used metaphorically (Mizutahi, 3). In his works, Bhabha comes up with a number of tenets about hybridity and fixity:

Hybridity Characterized by Reconciliation and Flexibility

Bhabha suggests that whereas the two essentialist groups are fixed and hostile, hybridity is agreeable and open to change. These two features of hybridity owe to its appeal to negotiation that entails fair exchange of values in win-win fashion. The colonizer and the colonized influence each other. In *Location of Culture*, Bhabha writes: "[i]t is in the emergence of the interstices-the overlap and displacement of domains of difference that inter-subjective and collective experiences of nationness, community interest or cultural value are negotiated," (2).

New Attitudes and Principles Evolve at the Third Space.

The hybrid is a more advanced mutant than the rigid essentialist. The negotiation involves exchanges that transform the hybrid. Bhabha observes that the hybrid being in a liminal space is in advantageous position because something new begins (2). New attitudes and value systems are formed that make the hybrid better adapted to life's challenges than the essentialist groups.

Hybridity as Mode of Resistance.

Bhabha describes hybridity as a space that is exposed to contradictions and ambiguities. It is paradoxical space in that it is agreeable but an instrument of resistance. He writes, "[i]t initiates new signs of identity and innovative sites of collaboration and contestation," (Bhabha,1). On one hand, it collaborates because the immigrant shuns blanket denunciation of the dominant group and borrows some of their cultural practices. On the other hand, it a site of contestation because it is a mode of resistance. Bhabha expounds that the ambivalent nature of hybridity is disruptive to the essentialist dominant group. It renders worthless the long cherished prejudices of the dominant group, for instance, their hold on moral superiority and cultural purity is shattered. Bhabha notes, "[t]his disruptive temporalty disrupts the narrative of the western nation (1). Bosma Ulbe asserts that people of mixed descent are a threat to white prestige and a sign of degeneration for a dominant group (52-53). Although for Bhabha hybridity is not identical to mixed marriage, he implies that when migrants learn the ways of the dominant group, they will master their deepest secrets and then gain ground against them. The Indian presence in England has influenced the British diet. The British foreign secretary, Robin Cook remarked, "[c]hicken tikka masala is now Britain's true national dish not only because it is the most popular but because it is a perfect illustration of the way Britain absorbs and adapts external influences. Tikka is an Indian dish (Raj, 3). It is what Thomas Hardy explores in his novel, *The Mayor of Casterbridge.* Donald Farfrae outwits his opponent Michael Henchard because he knows his scandalous secret of auctioning his wife, Susan and daughter; there is power in mastering your enemy's secret. Ngugi Wa Thiong'o reiterates the same subject in *The River Between* in the character of Mugo wa Kibiro: Africans should learn the ways of the white man as a mode of resistance. He writes, "Mugo often said that you could not cut a butterfly with a panga. You could not spear them until you learnt their ways and movement. Then you could trap, you could fight back (20).

Hybridity Eludes Politics of Polarity

Bhabha (Cited from Ashcroft et al) suggests that hybridity reduces disharmony and hostility between minority and dominant group (209). In other words, it deals a blow to fixity thereby reducing cultural tensions between the two groups. It makes this possible because the Self has attributes of the Other and the Other has attributes of the Self. Bhabha observes that the "interweaving of elements of the colonizer and colonized challenges the validity of any essentialist cultural identity" (Meredith, 2). And by pursuing hybridity we elude the politics of polarity because we are similar to others.

Cultures are Hybrids

In "Commitment to Theory", Bhabha asserts that no single culture is pure because cultures emanate from borrowings. Africans, for intance, borrowed formal education and cash economy from Europeans. He writes, "[i]t is only when we understand that all cultural statements and systems are constructed in this contradictory ambivalent space that we begin to understand why hierachical claims to the inherent orignality and purity of cultures are untenable (9-23). Bhabha also notes that hybridity results into adaptation to change; on the contrary, fixity is regressive. Having won the struggle for freedom, the new nations embark on the creation of a national culture. They are now free to reinvent their cultural identity by realigning their national traditions to western modern forms of information technology, language and dress. They do not therefore lag behind. In "Cultural Diversity and Cultural Differences" (Cited from Ashcroft et al), Bhabha notes, "[t]he people are now the very principle of dialectical reorganization and construct their culture from national text translated into modern western forms of information and technonoly, language and dress" (208).

Bhabha's and Hall's concept of hybridity is significant to this study because it looks at the role of hybridity in textualising migrant identity formation and as a strategy of textual resistance. Hall's contemporary model is based on hybridity. It rejects binary opposition or hegemonizing identity proposed by cultural fixity. By emphasizing the changing or rather fluidity and heterogeneity of diasporic identity, and denigration of Return to original homeland, Hall is advocating integration of diaspora in the host community via hybridity. Bhabha's hybridity and the third space have considerable implications for reinventing of atheist/Muslim, Christian/Muslim relations in East Africa and among East Africa immigrants living abroad as depicted in Abdi's novels. It is also significant in reconstructing a sense of nationhood and identity in Eastern Africa, especially Somalia. They offer the possibility of a cultural politics that eludes a politics of polarity between hostile clans, Muslims and atheists, Muslims and Christians. Instead, they are centred on the adaptation and transformation of culture and identity predicated within a new inclusive postcolonial Muslim/secular, Christian community that seeks to reconcile and overcome the deeply rooted past antagonisms.

1.9 Research Methodology

Research design

The study employed narrative analysis qualitative design. Qualitative research design entails textual study in which data presented for analysis is collected from primary texts (in this case selected works of Safi Abdi). Data from secondary sources helped in comprehension and theoretical or qualitative analysis of primary texts. The materials were read, reviewed and selected depending on their pertinent contribution to postcolonial migration and strategies of resistance. Data from primary texts was collected by reading the narratives of migrant characters in Abdi's two novels.

Narrative analysis is a type of qualitative research design. Tim May observes that narrative analysis "views narratives as interpretive devices through which people represent themselves and their worlds to themselves and others" (see appendix 2). Narrative analysis design seeks to understand human experience and social phenomena (in this context migrancy and strategies of resistance) via form and content of stories. It uses field texts such as stories, journals, and interviews as units of analysis to understand the way people create meaning in their lives as narratives. The study proceeded by close reading of primary texts and secondary sources such as published written interviews of immigrants (in journal articles) to capture experiences of migrant characters and their strategies of resistance in western cities.

The researcher engaged in content analysis to study the two texts. In this method, detailed information about the phenomenon being studied is obtained and then attempts to establish patterns, trends and relationships from data gathered is made. Details about hybrid and fixed characters were gathered and their relationships with dominant group described before being compared and contrasted to determine a better strategy of resistance. The study was purely library based and data was collected from two primary texts for analysis.

Sampling Procedure

The two texts were deliberately sampled based on postcolonial migration, resistance strategies and author's origin. This consideration was intended at assisting the researcher to examine a kind of migration that creates minorities that move (from East Africa) to live at the margins of the dominant group in the West and how they resist discrimination. Texts that depicted migration of characters that could not settle in the West like Mohamed's *Black Mamba Boy* were rejected. Two texts were chosen to ensure ample sample size for selection of hybrid and fixed characters for analysis.

Data collection

The primary data for the study was collected by close reading of Abdi's *A Mighty Collision of Two Worlds (2002)* and *Offspring of Paradise (2004)* and making notes on hybrid and fixed characters.

Secondary Data

The study enriched primary data by studying, reviewing and selecting of scholarly, literary articles, refereed journals, books, projects and theses from online sources, Post Modern Library at Kenyatta University and University of Nairobi. Secondary data enriched the study with ideas on migration literature, for instance, hybridity, fixity or essentialism, identity and abandonment. It also highlighted strands of postcolonialism and other social science concepts like psychology for analysis and interpretation of data.

Data Analysis and Interpretation

A study of major concepts of postcolonial theory and features of migration literature guided the researcher in comprehending hybridity, fixity and characteristic themes of migration literature. Various strands of postcolonial theory guided the analysis and interpretation of data: Edward Said's orientalism expounded on cultural fixity by singling out the duality between migrant characters and the dominant hosts. Fanon's concept of nationalism and abandonment neurosis was crucial in analyzing ambivalence, fixity and hybridity among migrant characters. Bhabha's ideas were foundational in definition of migration literature and analysis of fixity and hybridity, and their role in identity formation. Hall's traditional and contemporary models helped in comprehending fixity, hybridity and identity. Spivak's work expounded the concepts of identity and representation (see appendix 3). Representation was pertinent in examining the author's representation of migrant characters and establishing a new area for further scholarship.

The researcher related these theoretical concepts to Abdi's two novels and identified migrant characters that employed hybridity (hybrid characters) and those that chose fixity (fixed characters). The relationships between hybrid characters and fixed characters with the dominant group were described and then compared and contrasted to determine a better strategy of resistance.

A study of migration literature scholars like Sten Moslund, Bhabha, Abdolali and Pourjafari established themes typical of migration literature: coping strategies (hybridity and fixity), ambivalence and adjustment, identity and abandonment and return. The researcher then discussed the themes in Abdi's novels and then compared and contrasted them with characteristic themes of migration literature.

CHAPTER TWO

Characterization and Author's Concerns

This chapter explores how characterization is related to the representation of core concerns of *Offspring of Paradise* and *A Mighty Collision of Two Worlds* especially in matters of migration, ambivalence, hybridity, abandonment and return and human identity. This chapter then concludes by interrogating the author's representation of coping mechanisms and how the author represents diasporic Somalis as they interact with the notions of home through their everyday experiences.

The chapter explores the concerns using migrant characters such as Anisa, Sayid Jibreel and Yusuf in *A Mighty Collision of Two Worlds* and Hana, Abdirahman, Mulki and Little Hirsi in *Offspring of Paradise*. Born and raised at Rako Island, an imaginary island in the East, Anisa is the heroine in *A Mighty Collision of Two Worlds*. Her father dies early and she is raised by her uncle Omar, according to the Islamic tradition, in spite of the cosmopolitan nature of Rako Island. Her uncle, Omar, takes her to St. Joseph Catholic Mission School at the island to acquire formal education, and Anisa unconsciously imbibes Christian habits. The principal and teachers at the Catholic Mission School conceal Christian Evangelistic motives, for instance, the principal says "[t]eaching is a weapon, one of the many hooks we put on for the sake of the Lord Jesus. To ensure a sphere of influence during the tender years of a child's development, we give to all. But if the child grows and is not affected, we drop the child for a more adaptable one," (16). Anisa becomes one of these 'adaptable' children at the school and she is singled out with Jane Philip, a Christian student, for an exchange program at Fairwood in the United States of America. Anisa's mother, Fatima, aware of the impact Western culture can have on a pubescent girl, sets herself against the trip to America. On the contrary, Uncle Omar, supports it, and observes that it will be the best learning environment: he says, "[i]t will be an enriching experience," (30). With her uncle's blessings, Anisa leaves for the United States to join a more secular, cosmopolitan and foreign community than Rako Island.

Sa'id Jibreel is a pious man who goes overseas and sticks to his ethnic traditions such that he holds Western culture in contempt. He despises the dressing of white girls and would not like Somali girls to emulate it, and when he returns to Rako Island, he starts a Non Governmental Organization that fights for the rights and freedoms of Muslims and reclaim the moderate Muslims into pure Islam. As far as he is concerned, the moderates are "Muslim hypocrites" who should be Islamized afresh (84). Another character who will feature prominently in this chapter is Yusuf, a Muslim cleric in the United States. He has established an Islamic Centre, fully furnished with the mosque and the library to act as the connection between the diaspora and the ancestral home. Whereas Anisa plays a significant role in depiction of cultural hybridity in this chapter, Yusuf and Sa'id bring out cultural fixity.

Hana is the heroine in *Offspring of Paradise* and is central in expressing fixity as a coping mechanism. Born in a well-to-do family, she is orphaned at eight years of age after the militia carries out a broad-day-light assassination of her father and she is forced into exile with the grand mother, Ayeyo, the only surviving relative. Grand mother says, "[t]he roof grew wings and flew off my head. A step into the door and Hana's father shatters like crystal glass," (84). Hana is easily welcome in the foreign country because the hosts harbour hidden motives to convert Muslim youth to Christianity. They have a Christian organization called carriers, which means those entrusted with the responsibility of carrying the gospel to unreached people in the world. Hana is faced with a choice between her ethnic traditions, and be discriminated forever in the foreign city or Christianity, and be integrated in the white community. At first, she vacillates between cultural fixity and hybridity thereby depicting ambivalence as a core issue of migration. Later on, she settles on cultural fixity by rejecting Helen's attempt to push Christianity down her throat. Helen is a reformed alcoholic, murderer and dedicated member of the carriers, tasked with the responsibility of converting Hana to Christianity.

Like Yusuf in *A Mighty Collision of Two Worlds*, Abdirahman is a Somali Muslim cleric determined to connect Somali diaspora to their ancestral land in *Offspring of Paradise*. As a duksi teacher, he teaches the children religion and Somali language. He starts adult classes to encourage Muslim youth that the civil war in Somalia is Allah's punishment for the laity's sins. Abdirahman plays a significant role in depiction of cultural fixity and identity as one of the major concerns of Abdi. Mulki is another crucial migrant character in this chapter. Unlike Hana who belongs to the ruling clan in Somalia, Mulki belongs to the clan that forms the militia to overthrow Siad Barre. The major challenge she faces is the polarity that projects itself within the family. Mulki's mother comes from the ruling clan but her sons hunt and kill her relatives. Mulki's attempt to dissuade them is unsuccessful, and astounds her further when one of his brothers, Abdullah, murders the father. Mulki is forced into exile where she becomes an interpreter at the refugee camp in the foreign city. Her liking for hybridity prompts Rune, the chief administrator of the camp, to appoint her as Hana's guardian. Little Hirsi is a young immigrant in the European city who chooses to convert to Christianity. He works with a Christian evangelical organization known as the carriers to influence other Muslim youth into conversion to Christianity. Hirsi is crucial to this chapter in the depiction of cultural alienation as the alternative mode of coping with discrimination overseas.

2.1 Safi Abdi's Concerns

Characterization in Safi Abdi's fiction assumes the Jamesonian narrative model that assumes a narrative as a "socially symbolic act". In his work, *The Political Unconscious*, Frederic Jameson takes on the view that literary creation cannot be divorced from its political context. On the contrary, he observes that "the political unconscious" works through all texts as a disrupting force that reveals a disconnection between a text's meaning (as defined in any other way) and the "repressed and buried reality" (20) of the essential history of class struggle. In other words, for Jameson, all texts are essentially "bothered by a historical reality that allows them that very expression, since it is a historical reality," (20), founded on animosity, avarice and self alienation. In the actuality of this model, Abdi has created migrant characters (with a bitter historical past) in the diaspora to explore a spectrum of concerns, delving into the way characters come in conflict with alien cultures and strive to negotiate their existence. In their struggle to coexist in discriminative settings, Abdi thematises coping strategies, ambivalence, hybridity, and abandonment and return, as elaborated below.

2.1:1 Coping Strategies

In the two novels, migrant characters choose, with varying degrees of success, between cultural hybridity and cultural fixity in copying with discrimination in diasporic spaces. Some characters choose hybridity by occupying what Bhabha calls "the in between space" that enables the discriminated individual characters to occupy a middle ground between what is not wanted and what they want to achieve. Sten Moslund also observes that hybridity is "a process of intermixture or doubling of two or more cultures" (4). By this he implies that hybrid characters that stand at the third space embrace both attributes of the dominant group and the immigrant group and so inhabit the ambivalent site, which is socially enabling. Going by Moslund's definition of hybridity, the title *A Mighty Collision of Two Worlds* suggests "the intermixture" and clash of civilisations. There is therefore need for a middle ground where characters can coexist. Samuel Huntington in his book, *The Clash of Civilizations,* observes that "conflict between civilisations will be the latest phase in the evolution of conflict in the modern world," (22). He defines civilization as "the highest cultural grouping and broadest level of cultural identity" (23), for instance, the European community shares certain features that distinguish them from the Arabs and Chinese. For Huntington, there are eight different civilisations in the world today: Japanese, Confucian, Hindu, Islamic, Western, Slavic Orthodox, Latin American and African civilization. He asserts, "[t]he most important conflicts of the future will occur along the cultural fault lines separating these civilizations," (25). When Muslim immigrants like Anisa migrate and settle in the West, they pave way for the clash between the Islamic and Western civilizations. Huntington elaborates that post colonial migrations increase interactions among people of different civilizations, which "intensify civilization consciousness and awareness of differences between civilizations," (25). The civilization consciousness in turn heightens the tension between the different groups which may result in violent conflicts. To avert possibilities of violence, Anisa accommodates the alien culture and discredits the identity of stability and belonging such that she loves Mike, a white man and marries him. Their love relationship begins while they are in college, where they arrange dates and attend discos. Although Anisa is a Muslim, she unconsciously employs Christian strategies to spread Islam. Christianity, not "Islam, allows women to spread the religion" (496). Anisa influences Mike to become a Muslim by buying him books and taking him to Yusuf, a Muslim cleric. As the story comes to a close, Anisa observes that she, the aborigine of the East and Mike, "the drifting Westerner, are one and the same" (492). Both Anisa and Mike have embraced each others religion and so this fusion or intermixture destroys the narrative of religious essentialism, which deflates the possibility of conflict. She tells Mike:

> Your journey together with this person will be a very pleasant one. You guys can have the finest and brightest Christmas tree in the neighbourhood. What a cheer to your old mother. With this person, there won't be no more mountains to climb. No more reading of brain jostling stuff. You won't have to get wiser at all by reading heavy stuff. The two of you can read all the books in the world and yet remain the same simple souls forever. (461-462)

In the above passage, Anisa implies that her hybrid condition has moved a notch higher to overcome every temptation to fixity and accept the white community as they are. She is prepared to coexist with the whites, their difference notwithstanding; Anisa would cherish her ethnic traditions and let her Christian relatives celebrate their Christian traditions without judging them. Abdi suggests that coexistence is a process bedeviled with many challenges but with patience, it eventually succeeds; Nora, Anisa's neighbor at Rako Island, for instance, observes that their marriage is a predicament. She wonders why after a full day's talk, not a word has been mentioned about a reunion. They have had what Nora describes as "marriage one" (the civil marriage), "marriage two" (the Islamic wedding), "an abduction and counter abduction". She concludes that, " their problem should be send to the United Nations Security Council because theirs is a United Nations Union," (474).

The marriage between Anisa and Mike is a metaphor of cultural conflict, which represents the challenges that confront hybridized communities in our contemporary society. Abdi also implies that in spite of these challenges, hybrid communities should not despair, which is why Anisa says, "[l]et us face it Mike. These sad stories do abound, unhappy memories, unhappy spouses, confused kids, husbands. Baby abductions. Angry husbands. Confused in- laws. We must be aware these collisions make neat families" (454). In the aforementioned excerpt, Abdi brings to the fore challenges of hybridity, for example psychological trauma and ambivalence among children. There are Abdi's characters who cope with discrimination by retaining their national traditions and rejecting foreign ways abroad. Although these characters aspire to live in a cosmopolitan world, they stick to their ethnic practices and it therefore undermines their possibility of living peaceably in a cosmopolitan society. *In A Mighty Collision of Two Worlds,* Sa'id goes to the West and from the first day chooses to practice Somali traditions. He rejects all social elements of Western culture such as dancing at disco joints, listening to music and detests the Western dressing style. Sa'id's wife, Faiza tells Anisa about Sa'id, "[t]he poor fellow hasn't even heard of Michael Jackson's latest Album [...] he's never set foot in a disco joint all those years in Europe," (84). Sa'id has so much passion for Somali traditions that he refers to American girls and those Somali girls that emulate them as "plastic copies of females," and when he returns home at Rako Island, in the East, he reprimands all characters that choose the middle ground in the cosmopolitan Island, calling them "Muslim hypocrites" (84). He is desirous of seeing all Somalis embracing Islam in all its purity. Yusuf, the American cleric that converts Mike to Islam, reveres his Somali traditions and denigrates the white hosts. Yusuf associates Somali culture with moral uprightness, chastity and propriety but the West, in his opinion, represents incest, bestiality, gayism, Zionism, pornography, crime and Hellenism. While interrogating Anisa to understand her white husband's attributes, he asks, "[n]o gambling record?" Anisa denies, "No gambling record." And he proceeds with a barrage of questions that bear negative insinuations: "No criminality of any sort? No sympathy for nudists, no history of incest?" (138). He therefore disapproves marriage between Somali girls and white men and underscores the teachings of the Quran against marriage to white atheists. He asserts that they are idolaters until they believe.

In *Offspring of Paradise*, Abdirahman, a Muslim cleric and Hana's Quranic teacher at the refugee camp (the wall) chooses cultural fixity to cope with the foreign culture. He dedicates his life to teaching Somali children to memorize the Quran to protect them against cultural alienation. He starts classes to teach Somali immigrants their national tradition and Islam is part and parcel of that tradition. Abdirahman encourages those disappointed by the war in Somalia to restore their faith in the religion by holding that it is God's retribution for their sins.

Helen, Hana's white Christian friend, distastes him because he grounds the immigrants in their culture.

Some characters deliberately or unconsciously choose alienation as a coping strategy abroad. *Encyclopaedia Britannica* defines alienation as "a state of feeling estranged or separated from one's milieu of work, products or self". Sidney Finkelstein defines alienation as a psychological phenomenon, "an internal conflict, a hostility felt towards something seemingly outside oneself, which is linked to oneself, a barrier erected which is actually no defense but an impoverishment of oneself," (7). The character exhibits resentment against others yet the source of the problem is within and hence harms oneself. Finkelstein is making a reference to internal fragmentation, which is reiterated by Erich Fromm who observes, "[t]he meaning of alienation is that process of feeling in which anyone feels estranged from self," (10). Karen Horney observes that a person is alienated whose, "spontaneous individual self has been stunted, warped or choked, he is said to be in a condition of alienation from himself or alienated from self," (11). In her other work, *Our Inner Conflicts*, Horney defines a self alienated person as "a person simply becomes oblivious to what he really feels, likes, rejects, believes in short to what he really is," (12). He ignores his real self yet "man's reality is his real self" (13), and so estranging oneself from "the real self" is self alienation.

In *Offspring of Paradise*, Hana cuts loose from her guardian, Mulki and joins Helen's company. Hana becomes hostile towards Mulki, avoiding her all day round yet there is no offence Mulki has committed against Hana. She has an internal conflict probably stemming from the bitter history of polarity among her people, which caused the demise of innocent people like Zahra (Mulki's classmate who hails from Hana's clan), Hana's father and uncle. Hana is unconsciously anxious about having to live in a foreign land in absence of her grand mother, without her mother, without those with the ability to teach her the ways of her people. As Horney asserts, Hana becomes "oblivious" of what she likes, rejects and the reality of who she is. She falls in love with Helen's company, Helen is a female carrier tasked with the responsibility of evangelising to Muslim youth. Hana is self alienated because she deliberately ignores her real Muslim self, estranging herself from the real Muslim she is, which amounts to alienating herself. Usman, Helen's ex-friend, tells Hana to avoid Helen's company because it would be detrimental to her faith and learning. Hana warns Usman against dissuading her, saying unlike Usman "at least Helen has aims in life". She wonders, "[w]hat is a Somali man's aim in life [...]" (229). Hana's assertion that she 'would bury her head in shame' had she been a Somali man is contempt for her fatherland and a denial of who she is. The hostility towards her people is in Finkelstein's terms the "impoverishment of herself" because she sustains psychological sickness later in the story. She says, "[b]rave Somali brother, where was your bravery when your brothers dumped me here in this cold?" (230). As Horney puts it, her Muslim self is "stunted, choked and warped" by the violent background and the mosaic of culture in her new cosmopolitan environment. The white Christian hosts, for instance, know everything about the search for her mother but Mulki, her Somali guardian, knows nothing about it. Worse still, she boasts of writing her diary "in my version, not the tribal lore, not in the warlord's version," (237), a style absolutely inconsistent to the Somali tradition. This assertion signifies the shame and resentment she holds for her culture and underscores rootlessness and estrangement. Sam Lackland elaborates how alienation affects immigrant children in the United States of America:

Growing up in a society where their parents' values apply to a minority group, these children can experience an acute sense of shame in practicing their parents' culture in a society where mainstream people have different values and norms. Nevertheless, to reject their parents and their norms can be painful and result in extreme emotional problems. The child may experience guilty feelings, anxiety and loneliness. On the other hand, rejecting the society and taking sides with the parents may also create another form of loneliness- alienation. (23)

Hana is ashamed of her parents' culture, rejects it and the consequence is "extreme emotional problems." When she is not with Helen, then she languishes in loneliness and anxiety. The later manifests in Hana via occasional tantrums whenever Mulki tries to ask her where she has been: "[i]f you must Know [...] I was having lunch with Helen," (100). Helen's rejection, while they are at the ranch, the Hunters, comes as a shocking realization that she still does not belong to the white society. She concludes that life in diaspora is not "a cushion" and the immigrant is just "a lone invasive plant forever doomed to be cut down to size," (276), Hana does not belong anywhere by now, she is cut off from her migrant community like a tree separated from its roots. Her return to Mulki is the beginning of the end of her alienation, which has caused her psychological trauma. The doctor diagnoses a psychological disturbance after her ordeal at the Hunters, where her white Christian friend, Helen, threatens to kill her for refusing to convert to Christianity. The doctor's notes reveal a "very disturbed young woman" in spite of her beautiful face (342). She tells the doctor that she does not understand adults "from country A to B" for those "who hurt her most are adults" (342). Helen's shift to cultural fixity is an astounding betrayal that heightens her internal conflict, she loses her appetite and scratches her body for lack of vitamins, and her psychological disturbance cannot permit her a settled frame of mind.

Anisa, the heroine in *A Mighty Collision of Two Worlds*, adopts alienation as a coping strategy abroad. Erich Fromm defines self alienation as the absence of self awareness or complete loss it. In his work, *Sane Society,* he asserts, "[t]he meaning of alienation is that process of feeling in which anyone feels alienation from the self," (10). He adds that the alienated person therefore gets alienated from society because the loss of self awareness alienates him. Anisa loses self awareness after living in the United States of America for awhile. The fact is that she a practicing Muslim who has to affirm her faith by Shahada, participate in Saum (fasting) during the holy month of Ramadhan, perform Salat (prayer) five times a day, and refrain from worldly pleasures as laid down in the Holy Quran. In Horney's view, the Islamic identity is Anisa's "reality" of which once is lost will result in Anisa's self alienation. Horney looks at self alienation as a consequence of becoming "oblivious of what one likes", or of doing contrary to what one "really is" (12). As Anisa attempts to seek for the middle ground, she loses her Islamic faith, first by forgetting salat (prayer), claiming that "she has so much else to do during the day," (49). She starts attending discos, which is inconsistent to both Somali and Islamic tradition. In her letters, she does not write a word about religion, something she had dearly cherished right from childhood through to puberty. Contrary to the demands of the Islamic tradition, she falls in love with a white atheist, Mike, a young man who has defied his father's Christian religion and chosen to live a secular life. Anisa's parents' attempt to dissuade her into rejecting the so called 'heathen' relationship is utter fiasco, she rejects Sayid Jibreel's hand in marriage with American assertiveness, and confesses, "[w]hat I've picked up (from the United States) is how to say simple No" (81). She is now reading from Floor's script by degrading the communal nature of the Islamic culture. Floor is her first white roommate at Fairwood School, USA. She tells Faiza that Africans "have no monopoly of truth," (95), and adds that even if her marriage goes wrong, she will perfectly "take care of herself". Furthermore, she stops wearing the hijab, saying that "wearing it is tough nowadays," (104), just to illustrate the extent to which she is fast becoming another person besides "her real self".

Few years into the marriage, Anisa undergoes internal fragmentation; her marriage is similar to Antoinette's marriage to Rochester in Jean Rhys' *Wide Sargasso Sea*. Rochester tells the readers that he does not love Antoinette, he is "thirsty for her" but that is not love. He feels little "tenderness for her" since she is just "a stranger" to him; a stranger who does not think as he thinks or feel as he feels," (78). Nevertheless, underlying the difference was the racial superiority that Antoinette's husband, Rochester, upholds. As a white man, he embraces the prejudices that his race holds towards the Mulattoes in the Caribbean, for instance, the divine status the whites had created for themselves. Rhys does not assign Rochester a name throughout the first part of the novel because as a white man, he is a 'god' entrusted with a responsibility of giving names to Antoinette, and judging her actions and conduct. For example, when she sings songs, he says, "for they (songs) haunted me," (76), and when she gives money to her relatives, it is extravagance. Sometimes she calls her Marrionetta, other times Antoinetta; Antoinette tells Christophine, her maid, that Rochester calls her "marionette", which is another word for a doll (127). Rochester's psychological condition is well defined by Horney: "[s]elf alienation arises when a man makes an 'ideal image' of himself in his mind that is other than his real self: there exists a gap between his idealized image and his real self," (13). Rochester has created an ideal world for him to judge and create another person out of his wife, Antoinette, an endeavour that causes irreparable harm not just to the marriage but to Antoinette's psyche. These are the same experiences that Anisa and Mike pass through in *A Mighty Collision of Two Worlds* with Anisa taking Rochester's 'idealized image' to create another person out of Mike. She has crafted for herself an elevated state of moral and religious sphere that whatever effort Mike makes, she cannot see the ideal Muslim husband prepared to lead the family in the ways of Allah. She sees Mike as an amateur who only prays in the presence of the clergy; consequently, like Antoinette in *Wide Sagasso Sea*, she runs mad and is confined at the psychiatrist owing to "inner turmoil" (188). After discharge, the 'idealized image' proliferates, alienating Anisa from herself and Mike. She heaps all the blame on Mike and introduces tougher Islamic rules to 'recreate' him; she fails to 'recreate' Mike. Anisa abducts the children and flees to Rako Island.

Alienation distinguishes itself as the root cause of Anisa's predicament in *A Mighty Collision of Two Worlds*. Abdi suggests that immigrant characters are cut off from their mother cultures and lose their sources of life, which limits their chances of survival. Citing Albert Camus, Abdul Saleem sums up the fate of immigrant characters as a lost people: "[c]ut off from his religious, metaphysical and transcendental roots, man is lost; all his actions become senseless, absurd and useless (21).

Little Hirsi in *Offspring of Paradise* copes with foreign environment by alienation as a strategy of resistance against discrimination abroad. Fanon in his book *Black skins, White Masks* observes that when a weak willed negro makes contact with the white community, what ensues is "an ego collapse" and the goal of his behavior forthwith is to please the white man (154). Fanon refers to this as "abandonment neurosis" and is evident in Little Hirsi. When he arrives abroad, he betrays the Somali people by working so very closely with carriers, Christian Evangelists, to convert the Muslim youth in the refugee camp to Christianity. Helen, one of the carriers, is so proud of him and says, "[h]e is now one of us, free and frank," (147). At a certain stage of their systematized, Evangelistic mission, they introduce him to Hana, to bolster her confidence in the carriers. Hirsi gives a rote testimony of how he is a reformed murderer, robber and drug addict; he tells Hana that "his hands bazooka-ed" many people to "shrapnel" (197). Although he reveals that he has never converted to Christianity, Hirsi has already committed acts tantamount to betrayal of his fellow Muslim immigrants at the *Wall* such as risking Hana's life by working in cahoots with Helen, the manic. Had Mrs. Grant not assisted her, Hana would have been murdered by the sick carrier whose sole source of happiness lies in Hana's conversion.

On receiving this sad news of Helen's attempt to murder Hana, Hirsi apologises belatedly and singles out desperation as the cause of his alienation and decision to work in cahoots with the enemies of his people. He says, "I was a very desperate man when I met these people," (344). He has traded his people for money, favours and other material possessions as ways of coping with challenges overseas. Nonetheless, the hosts have never accepted him; they still arrest and lock him up for suspected robbery just because he is black. He tells Abdirahman he was "just passing by" when the police arrested him. Like Mugo in *A Grain of Wheat,* even when he tells Thompson, the white District Officer, that he knows the whereabouts of Kihika, the white man punishes him because he believes all black people are liars.

He says, "[t]he African is a born actor, that is why he finds it easy to lie," (54). Abdirahman wonders why Hirsi is out late in the night; he is arrested in the wee hours in the night at a crime scene. Hirsi reveals that he is sick; he is a victim of insomnia, which is symptom of psychological disturbance. "I am a night owl," he says, "sleep evades me, so I loiter a lot at night. It has been my routine," (346). Hirsi's psychological disturbance springs from his loneliness or disconnection from friends and family.

Loneliness is a form of alienation because it results from lack of intimacy with others. Herbert McClosky observes that "the feeling of loneliness and yearning of supportive primary relationships are two sides of a coin", (15), he defines loneliness as the loss of significant relation with others" that generates a source of "alienation called social isolation" (15). Hirsi's association with carriers has cost him meaningful intimacy with Somali immigrants and the physical separation from his immediate family deprive him of the warmth that gives him the peace of life. With insomnia, he finds the house dreary, bed worthless and ends up in the street at night to pass time like an owl. The image of the owl is a symbol of loneliness on one hand, evil on the other. Hana is very suspicious of Hirsi's integrity. In Hana's opinion, Abdirahman's decision to ask Hirsi why he "is out so late" shows how little he "knew about Hirsi's life," (345). Hana insinuates that Hirsi seeks sexual partners in town at night as a remedy to his social alienation that deprives him the joy of life. Hana, Anisa and Hirsi choose alienation as a coping strategy abroad with no chances of success; in fact they all sustain psychological sicknesses.

2.1:2 Ambivalence

Our world has conflicting situations that can be surprising, for example, a father loves his children and punishes them when they do wrong. There is a contradiction in this since love is a strong feeling of affection but punishment entails inflicting pain to discourage unwanted behavior. Both Christianity and Islam assert that God is all merciful and beneficent; however, He punishes His faithful who err against him. Michael Billing observes, "[c]ommon sense contains conflicting and opposed themes or values, for instance, people should be merciful and justice should be dealt," (238-240). Billing expounds that these conflicting situations, otherwise referred to as ambivalence, give rise to dilemmas. Dagmar Meyer observes that changes such as globalization and circulation of knowledge via internet "are producing conditions of profound uncertainty" in interpretation of ethics and social practices (2). Meyer implies that migrant characters that face the world with the knowledge of two worlds have this "profound uncertainty" in interpretation of the world overseas. Bauman Zygmunt asserts that "the postmodern habitat is a territory subjected to rival and contradicting meaning bestowing claims hence perpetually ambivalent," (193). Bauman's "postmodern habitat" is the world of Somali immigrants living in a place of rival cultures with claims of superiority, poised to outdo each other. Confronted by the duel between the two worlds, the characters get into a dilemma.

The origin of the term, ambivalence, is unclear. It comprises the latin prefix ambi derived from ambo, which means 'both'. The Oxford Dictionary defines ambivalence as duality of opposed emotions, attitudes, thoughts or motivations, which a person simultaneously bears towards another person, object or something. The person possesses both love and hate for something. Macmillan English Dictionary defines it as a feeling of different things about something or someone at the same time, for example, feeling that you like them and dislike them.

Ambivalence, according to Abdolali and Poujafari, is a "confrontation between two opposing affections" (688). They observe that migrant characters vacillate between love and hate for the two cultures: "[a]t one point desiring to retain cultural roots while at the same time being drawn to accept the new culture" (688). In Abdi's novels, there are characters that vacillate between Somali tradition and Western culture to depict the dilemma typical of ambivalent identities in migration literature.

In *A Mighty Collision of Two Worlds,* Anisa adopts Western culture from the outset. She rejects her father's culture and tells Uncle Omar that the only semblance between her and her father is appearance. She says, "[h]e was different," (102). She falls in love with Mike, an irreligious white man, and claims that "he can be a better Muslim" than Feiza (95). Soon after marriage, she shifts her ground and viciously attacks Western culture: she forbids Mike eating pork, he has to use water in the loos; he should not take breakfast in bed, and a host of many other rules. The reader is left to wonder where Anisa's loyalty belongs. The marriage suffers separation when Anisa flees to their home, Rako Island with the children; Mike comes later stealthily and abducts the children, an act that infuriates Anisa. Back at Rako Island, she tells her people the weaknesses of Western culture. She talks of the worldliness and hypocrisy of the West. She says the vacant looks in the eyes of the whites "told tales of humans who saw nothing beyond the limited life they now led- chronic diseases, coupled with the specter of death and awaiting an end they mocked during their reckless years and thought would never come," (276). Anisa attacks the West's contempt for religion and elevation of what she considers "worldliness", which ushers the whites into spiritual darkness. She claims that whites have placed their faith in tranquilizers and painkillers. At the end of the story, when Mike returns with children, Anisa does not show any hatred for Western culture. Instead, she says she will neither interfere with Mike's habits nor ask a silly question. Mike's "fridge can go back to life with "all things forbidden," (469), a reference to all kinds of alcoholic drinks and that he will still live peacefully with Anisa. She then digresses into fixity by attacking the whites, that they "do not talk straight; they are racists," (469). They just smile as a fashion, in fact they smirk, "[w]hen they smile, you smile back. When they say green, learn to say yellow. When they say black, say white. When they snub, you snub back", (469). These remarks are an affront to the very whites with whom Anisa has just pledged to coexist a few moments before; she vacillates, she is quite unpredictable, which is a clear indication of the conflicting emotions in her. Ambivalent as she is, it is not surprising to see her wedding Mike afresh at Rako Island. In fact, Mike relocates from the United States to Rako Island. At one point, Anisa asks for tissue paper for use in the loos, "Mike Paterson, have you by any chance any tissue paper? Not some poor quality ones that stick on people's faces, but good first class ones," (512). Apparently, Anisa displays a loving hate for the West, which is ambivalence.

In *Offspring of Paradise*, Hana, the heroine of the story, exhibits ambivalence like Anisa. Hana goes to a class dominated by white children and also joins a Christian service comprising of white and black pupils where she enjoys fellowship but when the priest "dropped a round flat chip into her mouth" (the Christian sacrament), " she spat the wetted stuff into a paper napkin," (150). Hana loves fellow white children and keeps Christian friends but when one of them calls her 'dark skull', she vents her anger by kicking a chair with her "bad winter boots", amid insults like "bad wood," (76), until the leg comes off. Already, Hana is vacillating between love for alien culture and hatred for it. Her request to "want" to "learn everything and anything" about her people's past (83), from the grand mother is evidence of the love for her ethnic traditions. She yearns for a rediscovery of herself in the past. In an argument with her white friend Helen, Hana dismisses her criticism by saying the animosity in Somalia is a simple instance of sibling rivalry. Hana turns down Helen's offer of house to move away from Mulki and sticks with the latter. Helen gets embarrassed when Hana tells her that in spite of polarity, Somalis "are family" in foreign countries (143). But when Usman, a Somali immigrant who had just denounced the carriers, comes to warn Hana about the risks of keeping Helen's company, she defends Helen passionately, shocking the reader by describing her as her "helper and friend" whose advice is law; in it she does not "read anything sinister," (228). She approves Helen's friendship and degrades Somali men saying, "[b]ravo, brother! The kind of brother we could all depend on. Where was your bravery when your brothers dumped me here in this cold?" (280).

At this instance, Hana rejects her people and chooses the West, represented by Helen; she even vouches that "not a single Somali ever cared" about her mother or her. She tells Abdirahman that Somalis "killed everyone that ever meant anything" to Hana (233), and hence do not deserve to know any good news from her. Nevertheless, when Helen plays a documentary insinuating that Africans are violent, Hana jumps to their defense. She contends that although Christian soldiers in Serbia are savage and barbaric, the world does not produce documentaries to expose them. The remark is an affront to the very whites she has just been shielding against Usman's criticism; as a result, the reader is left to wonder where Hana belongs.

2.1:3 Identity

Charles Taylor defines identity as "an understanding of who we are," (34), which he insists has to be determined by the other. Simon Clarke observes that cultural identities are marked by "race, ethnicity, gender and class," (511). In Abdi's novels, cultural identity of immigrant characters is marked by race and ethnicity. Some immigrant characters struggle with the identity question, in the maze of cultures in the new cosmopolitan world. In *A Mighty Collision of Two Worlds,* Anisa suffers an identity crisis in the face of Western culture. A few years after arrival in the West, she starts abandoning her Somali-Islamic identity and imbibes many aspects of Western culture. She marries an atheist, which is at variant with Somali traditions. As the marriage proceeds, the two identities: Islamic and Western clash and Anisa becomes a psychological wretch. Her traditional Somali identity reasserts itself against the somewhat alienated self. The former self does not forgive the hybrid self for desecrating Islam. She tells the white doctor that she victimized herself, "imitating the ignorant folk," (223). The reprimanding voices that condemn her as she leaves the hospital are those of the "traditional" Islamic identity that the narrator describes as a "Stone Age specter that had lived long ago and knew everything," (227). It is Anisa's original identity that Hall describes as "traditional and shared," (393). Anisa yearns for a return to the fixed essence, which Hall questions. It is kind of identity that prides in its traditions and condemns other cultures. No wonder Anisa argues that she had a "perfect way of life but defiled herself by consorting with the pagans of the world," (223).

Mike is the pagan that has come in Anisa's life to adulterate what she deems perfect and lead her in to Satan' s ways of life, this thought heightens guilt in her heart. After discharge from the hospital, she renounces her hybrid identity and chooses the traditional, fixed identity. She tells Mike that she is prepared to "rid herself of all duplicity," (235). This is a rejection of double identity in favour of fixed identity. She goes back to wearing the scarf, which embarrasses Mike; he wonders why "she attracts attention to herself," (235). Anisa replies that she has now restored her, Islamic identity: "I am not letting go of me. This is natural me," (236). Henceforth, she whole heartedly embraces Islam in all its purity and demands that Mike does the same or forfeit the marriage. Mike tells her that it is her vacillation between identities that instigates insanity. The realization that in her hybrid state, the special Muslim she was is no better than Mike, the 'drifting Western soul' and 'pork eater' astounds her beyond description.

In the last chapters of *A Mighty Collision of Two Worlds,* it is very clear that Anisa has two identities: the former and current self. Having attained a higher degree of hybridity, Anisa looks at the traditional identity as another self. She tells Mike while at Rako Island: "[t]his person will never embarrass you by asking silly questions about mouse holes and tiny balls. With this person, prayer mats shall be a thing of the past and the fridge could be back to life with all things forbidden," (461-462). The 'she' in the above excerpt is the hybrid identity Anisa has now attained to coexist with the West. The new identity will accept Western attributes that differs with her Islamic values. In *Offspring of Paradise,* most characters choose fixed identities. Abdirahman, Usman, Ayeyo, Mulki and Hana have a great reverence for their ethnic traditions. Hana chooses a hybrid identity to wrench herself from Mulki's surrogate parenting; as a result, she keeps Helen's company and the carriers even take her to church and expose her to Christian lifestyle, for example, watching the Jesus Film. Hana also dresses like white girls: "Blue pair of trousers, blue winter jacket and her long braided hair hangs on each side of the shoulders," (162). But when Helen coerces her to fully embrace Christianity, she rebels against her and reverts to a traditional identity. Unlike Anisa in the other novel, Hana rejects those habits that compromise her Islamic faith such as love relationships with white men. She refrains from orgies, drinking and visiting disco joints. In the church, she spits the sacrament which is a religious symbol of the Christian altar, forbidden in her Islamic faith. She interacts with the carriers but sticks to her prayers to preserve her traditional identity.

2.1:4 Abandonment and Return

Abdolai and Poujafari observe that migrant writers recount diverse humiliation they suffer when seeking sanctuary overseas (689). As a result, they desire to return to their mother culture, a claim reiterated by Fanon in *Black skin, White Masks*. In the sixth chapter entitled, "[t]he Negro and psychopathology", Fanon investigates the extent to which Freud's and Adler's conclusions can be applied to understand the black man's view of the world (141). He observes that both in Africa and Europe, the family in which a child grows is a microcosm of the outside world hence there exists a close connection between the structure of a family and that of a nation. He writes, "[t]he family is a miniature of a nation, the centralization of authority in a country automatically entail a resurgence of authority of the father," (142). As a child leaves the authority of his parents he meets a replication of same laws and principles in the outside world, subsequently, a healthy child brought up in a healthy family in Europe and Africa will be a normal adult. To emphasize this observation, Fanon cites Heuyer:

For the individual, the authority of the state is the reproduction of the authority of the family by which he was shaped at childhood. Ultimately, the individual assimilates all authority that he meets to the authority of parents: he perceives the present in terms of the past. Like all other human conduct, behavior towards authority is something learned. (142)

For Fanon, children who have submitted to familial authority whether from Africa or Europe have potential to submit to the authority of any other state in the world. However, the contrary is the case among black people. He writes, "[w]e observe the opposite in the man of color. A normal negro child having grown up within a normal family will become abnormal on the slightest contact with the white world," (140). This is a shocking revelation, which Fanon proceeds to unearth the root cause. Citing Dr. Breuer and Freud, he attributes the black man's queer behavior to abandonment neurosis:

In almost every case, we could see that the symptoms were so to speak like residues of emotional experiences to which for this reason we later gave the name psychic traumas. This trauma, it is true has been quite expelled from the consciousness and memory of the patient and as a result has been apparently been saved from a great mass of suffering but the repressed desire continues to exist in the unconscious; it is on watch constantly for an opportunity to make itself known and it soon comes back into consciousness but in a disguise that makes it impossible to recognize, that is the repressed thought that acts as surrogate and soon surrounds itself with all feelings of morbidity that have been averted with the repression in the unconscious. (144)

In the above text, Fanon suggests that the Negro buries his past experiences- the family and its traditions in the unconscious, but he has not eradicated them. It is 'the repressed desire' because; it is the culture he holds dear, the values he has upheld since childhood. In the unconscious, it is just waiting for an opportunity to explode and endanger the patient's mental health. This opportunity avails itself when the white society reveals that it does not value the black person however assimilated he is. The black man who joins the white privileges has abandoned his culture, as earlier hinted. Fanon observes that the individual negro who "climbs up into society- white and civilized- tends to reject his family- black and savage- on the plane of imagination" (149), he casts the family in the id but after interacting with the white hosts to whom he is now indebted, he recognizes the unreality of many of the beliefs that he has adopted with reference to the contemptuous attitude of the whites. The reality becomes extremely resistant, and since the Negro's inferiority or superiority complex is conscious, he is stricken by guilt and returns to his former self.

Fanon's abandonment neurosis is relevant to Abdi's heroines that reach the West and reject their mother culture, throwing it into the id. In *Offspring of Paradise*, Hana joins the privileged white society after her grandmother's demise. Torn between surrogate parenthood of a Somali from the rival clan and the guidance of Christian carriers, she opts for the latter. Hana hopes that hybridity would assign her identity for quick integration in the dominant community. In her friendship with Helen, Hana gives it all; she is sincere and honest, pouring her heart in it with clear knowledge that the carriers have noble intentions for her. Hana cannot bring herself to believe Usman when he criticizes Helen. She frankly tells Usman that Helen is a friend with better goals and sense of purpose than the likes of Usman. She is "a big sister, an invaluable confidante," (184), and sharer of her sorrows. In Fanon's view, the ways of her people are not eradicated; they are just repressed and searching for an opportunity to explode. The rejection of her culture is just a symptom of neurosis; Hana is sick as she climbs staves into the carriers' way of life. The reality starts dawning on her that she is just Helen's project.

The carriers use a systematic, manipulative form of hybridity and have made inroads into Muslim immigrants. Hana is tricked; Helen is carrying out "the waiting period," a stage which involves friendship building. "Ties are strengthened before favors are given," (185). With each of her dates, Hana's heart is drawn into irrevocable affection for a foreign culture. "Reorientation and gratitude" building process will follow "the waiting period" stage. Little Hirsi is then introduced to give credibility to the carriers' work. Hana thanks them for the support they give to Hirsi, "I really appreciate what you are doing for Little Hirsi," (186), they are supporting his whole family. When Hana takes a slow pace in imbibing Western values and Christianity, Helen threatens to use force. It dawns on Hana that she is supposed to pay back for the carriers' generosity with her own soul. Helen tells Hana, "[i]t is pay back time," (267), "we feed you, clothe you and you owe us your life. It is because of us that you are still alive," (270). These tirades deeply hurt Hana, it astounds her because Helen, "the sister" she trusted, betrays her.

Hana discovers that in fact, Helen is not a friend; she is just a proprietor of a project that has to be completed by hook and crook. Hana's previous decision to throw her family and Somali immigrants to the id to facilitate the entry to the white society is yet to give her an identity, overseas. To Helen she is just "a wretched immigrant forever doomed to be cut down to size," (276). Hana resolves to return to her repressed self, the traditional Somali values or fixed identity; perhaps this would assign her identity. She identifies herself with African Muslim immigrants to counter Helen's denunciations after noting what Fanon calls "the unreality of the new values she has adopted" (149). The psychiatrist that Hana visits at the end of the story diagnoses mental disturbances, which is evidence of abandonment neurosis in Hana's life.

In *A Mighty Collision of Two Worlds*, Anisa's rejects the culture of her people when she arrives in the West. In Fanon's view, she "casts them "into the id, (149), as she interacts with white people. The prayers, the Islamic code of dress and communal Somali way of life become parochial and backward to her. Anisa reminds us Fanon's observations: "[w]hen the Negro makes contact with the white world; a certain sensitizing action takes place. If his psychic structure is weak, one observes the collapse of the ego. The black man stops behaving as an actional person, the goal of his behavior will be the Other, for the Other alone can give himself worth," (154). Indeed, Anisa abandons the traditions of her people in spite of her white friends adjusting to accept her as she is. The narrator says that her roommate "Floor had come to accept what she termed her friend's bizarre habits," (49), but Anisa feels guilty. For example she prays "very fast like a thief for fear of being seen by others," (49). Forthwith, each of her actions is undertaken to please the West: going to disco joints, taking white boyfriends, all of which are a transgression of her mother culture. She represses the Somali tradition, as Fanon claims, and it awaits an opportunity to explode.

As soon as she expresses her superiority complex against her white in-laws, they fight back and the old self emerges from the unconscious to confront the alienated self. The neurosis is so acute and is made worse by the reality that she cannot abandon the Islamic traditions that formed the very foundation of her life such as salat (prayer), the shahada (affirmation of faith) and saumu (fasting); at the expense of the materialism and secularism of the West. The contest between her spiritual values (that assign her superiority) and the West strikes her with guilt; guilt so severe that she decides to return to her mother culture. Anisa places her matrimonial home under stringent Islamic rules; she coerces Mike to do everything like as Islam dictates for example, washing in the toilet with water and "washing hands before eating," (164).

In spite of her effort to convert her husband, Anisa realizes that the abandonment has dealt a big blow to her faith such that she cannot affirm it by uttering shahada. Guilt gnaws in her soul; she regrets having desecrated the holy faith that assigns her identity. Anisa feels that she has trampled on the very principles that make her who she is, that make her happy; that give her a reason to live. The guilt degenerates into severe neurosis that deprives her control of her faculties; Anisa is admitted at the psychiatrist's. Fanon describes this condition as "abnormality of the Negro when he comes in contact with the white society (46). Anisa's neurosis stems from the fear that she is in a lifetime companionship with a husband without spiritual enlightenment, "without capability to carry out the responsibility that comes with being Muslim," (185). Consequently, she compels Mike to accept/practice Islam to Rako Island.

Anisa's journey to Rako Island represents a search for a fixed or traditional identity. It is what Hall refers to as "passionate research" for fixed identities, an attempt to recover lost identity by returning to the original Africa. It also expresses Fanon's abandonment neurosis where during the first stages the African immigrant represses his traditional identity in a deluded belief that he is integrating but when reality dawns on him that he cannot fit in the white society, he retreats in a painful process of psychological trauma. The anxiety that gives her nightmares such that she has to shout the shahada to scare away jinnis reiterates Fanon's claim that "the Negro is phobogenic". Citing Charlies Odier, he asserts that "all anxiety from a certain subjective insecurity linked to the absence of the Mother," (46). Anisa's behavior exhibits extreme phobia for Western culture; like Bigger Thomas in Richard Wright's *Native son,* she sees whites as "a mysterious force" and he had "to carry a gun because he was going among white people" (81). For Fanon, the phobia owes to the absence of the mother. The mother represents the mother culture that she had earlier on rejected.

2.1:5 Polarity and Political Strife

Abdi foregrounds the devastating impact of polarity between the marginalized group and dominant group in a cosmopolitan society. *Offspring of Paradise* depicts the ill-consequences of the politics of polarity to a community. Siad Barre, the leader of Somalia, favours his clan; he reserves high profile jobs for them in the civil service and segregates the other clans. The narrator observes that "the regime masterminded twenty years of corruption, depravity, mass killings and persecution," (56). These acts of impunity and subjugation compel the marginalised clans to start guerilla campaigns against the regime at Buro, Hargeisa and other parts of Somalia. The results of the subsequent political strife are tragic: first, there are arbitrary murders and assassinations. Hana's father is assassinated on the way to the mosque and the uncle, shot while vacating house. In an unfortunate turn of events, Abdullah, Mulki's brother, kills his own father: "bang,

Abdullah's loaded machinegun [...] exploded through the father's chest," (34). Abdi suggests that war has dehumanizing effect on the society. Abdullah is so engrossed in cultural fixity that he forgets the ties of blood he has with this father.

Abdi also observes that the political strife that stems from polarisation of a cosmopolitan society leads to annihilation of men. Given that it is men who face the brunt of war, they die in large numbers leaving behind widows and orphans. In satirical voice, Abdi writes "[a] widowed mother and her children, a widowed hen – mother and her six chicks and a widowed he-goat, two orphaned ewes, three widowed sheep" (54). In the story, we find many widows like Ayeyo (Hana's grandmother), Asha, (Hana's mother), Amina (Asha's friend) and Mulki's mother. As a consequence of strife and destruction of a nation, many citizens migrate from Somalia to seek for Asylum in the West. Hana's clan which is an offshoot of Siad Barre's clan is branded, fagash (loyalists) and persecuted by the militias. Many of them flee Somalia in droves. Mulki's father, having married from the ruling clan is persecuted and eventually murdered by his own son who is determined to avenge the suffering of his previously marginalized clan. Mulki and fellow refugee send up in the wall, a refugee camp also referred to as "Qashin-qub, garbage dumps for Somali fugitives," (10).

In *A Mighty Collision of Two Worlds* there is evidence of polarity between the Muslim minority and the secular group in the island after Sa'id's and Usman's detention. The latter's demand for an Islamic School and rejection of government funding does not go down well with the secular regime. The government perceives them as radical Muslims with "revolutionary ideas that ran contrary to mainstream currents" (285), hence a bad influence on the Muslim populace. For this reason; they arrest and charge them with drug peddling. The Rakon community is polarized along religious lines and the communities prepare for political upheaval. The personal secretary to the president appeals to hybridity to avert a crisis; whereas cultural fixity results in political strife in *Offspring of Paradise*, hybridity averts violence in *A Mighty Collision of Two Worlds*.

2.1:6 Cultural Conflict

Abdi depicts a clash between different cultures in the contemporary, cosmopolitan society. She reiterates Huntington's views that "civilizations clash because the differences among them are not only real but basic" (25), and they differ in terms of language, culture, tradition and most importantly, religion." He writes:

> The people of different civilizations have different views on relations between God and man, the individual and the group, the citizen and the state, parents and children, husband and wife, as well as differing views on rights and responsibilities, liberty and authority, equality and hierarchy. These differences are product of centuries and will not soon disappear. They are far more fundamental than differences among political ideologies and regimes. Differences do not mean conflict but over centuries, differences among civilizations have generated violent conflicts. (25)

In *A Mighty Collision of Two Worlds*, migration brings the Western and Islamic civilization in contact with each other. At the beginning, there is no conflict but as they interact with each other, there is "civilization consciousness" that start producing reactions on either side of the divide. The "two worlds" in the title is reference to Islamic and Western civilizations that clash owing to their organic differences, for example, Americans, like Mike, cannot understand why there can be war among countries that profess Islam yet Islam is peace. Mike asks, "[i]f Islam means peace, why the absence of peace in the Muslim world? Why the absence of peace in this half Muslim home?" (158). Anisa explains the concept of peace as handed down in Islam: "the peace is only for those who truly follow Islam" (158), and better still, it is a personal peace, the peace of mind and heart. Anisa therefore implies that those who do not obey Islam to the letter like Mike and herself cannot get the peace. Mike also questions the position of women in Islam. In his Western eyes, women should go without veils and so Muslim women are under oppression. He tells Anisa that "the only freedom Muslim women have in Islam is found only in books," (159).

However, Anisa sees the treatment of women in Islam as fair and acceptable because Islam has assigned them their rights and responsibilities, which men have to abide by. Anisa suggests that Muslim women cannot just be subjected to unlawful acts of violence as Mike imagines; any punishments are meted out according to demands of Islamic laws. This is what she means when she tells Mike that "there are no subjugated battered women," (159), in dire need of protection by the West. The veil and the Muslim scarf, sheer symbols of submission among women in the East, are interpreted as symbols of oppression in the West; hence is the clash of two worlds. When Anisa starts wearing them after leaving hospital, the white people in town cannot "pass by without first staring at her," (233), even Mike has to keep a safe distance from Anisa.

Whereas the West sees individual sexual orientation such as homosexuality and lesbianism as a human right, but the East counts them as abominations that should be severely punished. Westerners' democratic culture is deeply entrenched in the society, underscoring respect for individual rights and freedoms, including gay rights. Easterners like Yusuf, the Muslim cleric, see such Westerners as sexual perverts. He asks Anisa whether Mike is "incestuous, gay, nudist, pork eater, and dog lover," (139), all of which he disapproves. Moreover, the West has for centuries build a materialistic culture which emphasizes material possession as the bottom line of happiness. Mike asks Anisa why "there are far many poor people in the Muslim world" (158), if Islam is peace. Anisa replies that "money isn't all" (159), and that Muslims have spiritual endowments that are much better than material wealth. Whereas in the West, a husband is any man who has the material wealth to provide for the wife and children, the East demands that a husband be a custodian and teacher of religious values to the children. Anisa's marriage depicts this clash with stunning clarity. However much Mike tries to please his wife, he cannot meet the Eastern standard of morality she has set for him. Her image of the ideal man is that with ability to lead the children to the unadulterated Islamic ideal. Mike "is a non-believer in his father's faith" (185), and therefore has no religion to hand down to their children (185). She finds her growth in the Islamic religion too slow to meet the standard of a Muslim marriage. Anisa decides to abandon "the almost heathen" marriage.

In *Offspring of Paradise* Hana finds some aspects of the Christian religion absurd, particularly the Christian concept of salvation. She is shocked to understand that Helen worries herself so much just because Hana has refused to convert; it stuns her to learn that Christians believe they have a bounden duty to save the world. She asserts that Rune, Jason, Helen, the young master and others "converge on the Muslim youth" to convert them (349). Helen, for instance, "hungered for a perfect world where everyone was happy and none was wronged," she therefore saw Hana and fellow "immigrants as the most wronged generation," (439). Hana betrayed her by refusing to become a Christian, to enjoy the happiness thereof. She is so elated to play the Jesus film, talk of how "the Lord saved her, Jason, Little Hirsi and is ready to save Hana for free" (265); Hana does not understand it because Islam does not uphold salvation from sin by "a son of God who was crucified". Perhaps Helen would have taken sometime to explain to Hana. She feels ambushed by her demand to "get saved", she feels compelled to watch films she does not like. It is no simple matter; like Jesus, the father of Christendom, Helen is ready to sacrifice her life for the sake of Hana. Abdi writes, "Little Hana is and has been Helen's favorite case since she dropped from heaven," (267). Helen is so determined to have Hana saved that if she loses it, she loses her life.

According to the Christian culture, Helen is an exemplary Christian evangelist but for her extremities: taking Christ's place in her evangelistic cause. Christians are encouraged to pursue souls and "save them from sin". In the book of Mathew of the Holy Bible, Jesus spoke to his disciples "to go and make disciples of all nations" (32). Hana, being a Muslim finds the concept of salvation distasteful and returns to her mother culture by opting for cultural fixity. Her flight from the Hunter's to Mulki's home is a rejection of cultural hybridity. In *A Mighty Collision of Two Worlds*, Abdi suggests that although cultures clash, they can still coexist at the middle ground. Anisa separates with Mike but later, they reconcile at the middle ground to signify coexistence. As the story comes to a close, she tells Mike that she will allow him "to fill the fridge with things forbidden," (462), bear with his pork eating and refrain from forcing him to pray. They wed afresh at Rako Island and their marriage proceeds at the middle ground where doubling and intermixture of cultures is possible.

2.2 Thematic Relevance to Migration Literature

Abdi's characters effectively depict thematic concerns; however, this project is not just concerned with any thematic concerns but those concerns typical of migration literature. This subsection will compare and contrast Abdi's thematic concerns with what literary scholars consider as themes of migration literature.

Abdolali and Poujafari define migration literature and underline concerns typical of migration literature. They refer to migration literature as "literature whose subject is migration and the culture of the host nation" (681). They emphasize that "expression of nostalgic feelings does not place a work of art on the corpus of migration literature," (681). Moslund observes that the twenty first century has "witnessed a massive defeat of gravity, immense uprooting of people from their original homelands, displacement of borders and all clashes between cultures," (2). As a result, migration has replaced traditional settler life. Expounding on Roy Sommer's novel, Moslund defines migration literature as "literature having the central theme of hybridity," (5). He notes that Sommer's use of the word 'transcultural' refers to hybridity, "which connotes cultural up-rootedness as opposed to fixity of homeland and rootedness of traditional works," (5). He points out that Sommer sees hybrid literature as "that involving dissolution of fixed cultural identities and accentuation of cosmopolitanism," (5). Moslund further emphasizes the fluidity of migration literature "encapsulating inbetweenness, borderlessness and transitory identities as inseparable part of the theme". His observations are based on Bhabha's hybridity and outline the salient characteristics of migration literature as "a new kind of art that depicts fluid identities that have replaced old identities of stability and belonging," (687). Here, "the fluid identities" he refers to is cultural hybridity, a space between the two essentialist groups, the ambivalent site where there is mixing and doubling of cultures, while "identities of stability and belonging" are a reference to cultural fixity. Basing their study of Bhabha and Moslund, Abdolali and Poujafari come up with themes typical of migration literature as follows:

2.2:1 Cultural Hybridity and Cultural Fixity

Abdolali and Poujafari observe that migrant writers create characters that cope with discrimination abroad by hybridity and fixity. They point out that some characters see "migration as a destructive, agonizing and painful experience," (686), which is cultural fixity because they are filled with nostalgia about their culture. Others see "migration as productive, fascinating and an opportunity to learn new things," (686); which is cultural hybridity. Pourjafari and Vahdipour observe that these two coping strategies assist in rewriting the cultural identities of the immigrant characters. Citing Bhabha, they underscore the importance of hybridity in the immigrant's life and that of the migrant writer. For Bhabha, "sticking to past cultures would bring about dangers of cultural fixity and fetishism of identities," (9). He singles out cultural fixity as the contrary to cultural hybridity and expounds that it eradicates new insights the writer needs to write about experiences beyond his borders. In Bhabha's view, the migrant writer reflects a cosmopolitan tradition in his work depicting neither "the superiority of his national culture nor ethical beliefs but a representation of the third space that is beyond essential groups," (13). Moslund refers to this "third space as the distinguishing theme of migration literature," which manifests itself via "cultural in-betweeness, of intermixture and fusions of two or more cultures" (4). He means that when characters migrate to foreign lands, some integrate by taking aspects of the dominant group, for instance, language, religion and intermarriage.

As observed in the previous subsection, Abdi is concerned with cultural hybridity and fixity in her two novels. Anisa and Hana go beyond their Eastern borders and vacillate between the two coping strategies to survive in the host nation. In *A Mighty Collision of Two Worlds,* Abdi represents a cosmopolitan tradition where there is equality between the East and the West. Anisa says there is no difference between her, the Easterner and Mike, the Westerner: "Anisa saw with her own eyes that she were in effect no better than Mike," (492), given that both have acquired attributes of the East and the West. In *Offspring of Paradise,* Hana chooses her national traditions over Western culture as a coping strategy. She rejects all temptations that threaten her Somali Islamic identity, including love affairs with white men. She disavows Helen's attempts to force her into Christianity and makes a symbolic Return to Mulki's patronage. However, some elements of Hana's conduct depict an in-depth mastery of Christianity and Islam, the East and West, which is a salient aspect of hybridity.

2.2:2 Identity

Bhabha observes that both cultural fixity and hybridity affect identity of immigrants in the host nation. He notes that although Fanon recognizes the importance of "subordinated peoples" (immigrants) asserting "their indigenous traditions, he is aware of fixity and fetishism of identities," (9). Whereas for Fanon, personal maturity (identity) is by "clinging to ethnic traditions", (8), Bhabha advocates hybridity, a space where the migrant recreates himself by encountering cultural complexities and discrimination. He adds that it is "the third space that establishes a bridge between the immigrants' home and the world. There are cross-cultural initiations that establish a new identity," (9). By "cross-cultural initiations", he refers to interactions between minorities and the dominant group, which produces a new mutant, a person with new values. Abdi depicts the theme of identity as laid down by Bhabha and migrant literature scholars. She creates immigrant characters that determine their identity by fixity and hybridity. There are migrant characters like Abdirahman, Usman, Sa'id, Yusuf, Khadija and Hana who settle for fixity and others like Anisa, Mike, Uncle Omar, Little Hirsi and the personal secretary who chooses hybridity in her novels as elaborated in the previous subsections.

2.2:3 Ambivalence and Adjustment

Abdolali and Poujafari define ambivalence "as the conflict between two opposing affections in the life of the immigrant," (687). They add that the resolution of the struggle is achieved when the immigrant adjusts to the environment by choosing the middle ground. Migrant characters fluctuate between identities experiencing a desire to retain cultural roots while at the same time drawn to integrate in the new culture.

Nicholas Dirks observes that culture is a "multiple competing discourse" and it is difficult for characters to maintain fixed identities in a cosmopolitan setting. He writes:

> Neither culture itself nor the regimes of power that are imbricated in cultural logics can ever be wholly consistent. Identities may be seen as attempts to create coherence out of inconsistent cultural stuff [...] but every actor carries around enough contradictory strands of knowledge and passion. (18)

In the previous subsection, we discussed how Abdi's characters Like Anisa and Hana vacillate between their ethnic traditions and Western culture. For Dirks, they carry with them "contradictory strands of knowledge and passion" from the East and West. Meyer refers to the vacillation as "non identity" (2), given that the characters cannot identify themselves with a particular cultural group. Some migrant characters get extremely alienated in the process of adjusting to the alien culture and then strive to return to their mother culture.

2.2:4 Abandonment and Return

Abdolali and poujafari observe that "the theme involves description of the journey from the homeland to diaspora and the notion of return". It also explores "diverse experiences of the flight of immigrants and the humiliation they suffer from when seeking assistance" (689). In *Offspring of Paradise*, Abdi gives us a detailed description of Hana's and Mulki's journey from Somalia to Kenya and then to the refugee camp, the wall, overseas. She captures the difficulty of fleeing out of Hamar with Zahra, the fagash woman a journey that costs the life of both Zahra and Mulki's father. Other acts of humiliation of migrant characters are elaborated in the previous subsection of this chapter. Abdi also explores Fanon's concept of "abandonment neurosis" typical of black characters who visit Western cities. Both Anisa and Hana reject their culture as they interact with white society. Fanon describes it as "repression," (144), as opposed to eradication. When they come face to face with the bitter reality of their "resolution," that is, constant rejection, they realize the importance of their own traditional values and the old self asserts itself. There a clash between the old and new self and the result is "psychological trauma".

Save for cultural conflict and political strife, the rest of Abdi's concerns are typical of migration literature namely: hybridity, ambivalence, identity and abandonment and return. Her novels meet the criteria of migration literature since their subjects are migration and the culture of the host nation. Hana and Anisa strive to adjust in the secular and Christian traditions of the West. There is also an attempt to dissolve fixed identities and accentuate cosmopolitanism as proposed by Moslund. There is fusion of Christian, Muslim and secular characters in *Offspring of Paradise* and *A Mighty Collision of Two Worlds*. Moslund's "transitory identities" are well explored in the next chapter. Abdi's heroines fluctuate between their mother culture and Western culture.

2.3 Abdi's Representation

In her essay, "Can the Subaltern Speak?" Spivak cross-questions the notion of representation in post colonial studies. She postulates that the subaltern is so "irretrievably heterogeneous" that the writer may not have the capability to represent them perfectly (78-80). Spivak gives the British example in which in the attempt to represent the Indian widow by banning the sati rite, the British end up silencing Hindu traditions. To what extent does Abdi represent the Somali immigrants given their heterogeneous nature? Does she in the process of representing them end up silencing some of them? This sub-section will analyse Abdi's concerns and interrogate the extent of her representation. Abdi depicts a number of coping strategies that migrant characters employ overseas. In both novels, she singles out hybridity as a coping strategy. In *A Mighty Collision of Two Worlds*, Anisa reverts to hybridity after futile attempts to employ fixity; her return to hybridity is meant to save her marriage. By her choice of hybridity, Abdi implies that it is the most appropriate strategy migrant characters should choose to coexist in a cosmopolitan environment. She tells Mike that at the middle ground, their life will be a pleasant one because she will allow him "to stuff the fridge with things forbidden," (462), she practices her religion. Towards the end of the story, she observes that she is just the same as Westerners. She asks Mike to give her tissue paper to use it. Anisa probably wants to use it in the washroom, which is inconsistent to the demands of Islamic tradition; the act depicts the degree of her hybridity. She has imbibed aspects of Western culture to minimize the difference and uphold diversity. By offering hybridity as a coping strategy, Abdi misrepresents some migrant characters. She silences those migrant characters with fixed identities. They revere their traditions and will not tolerate Western values. Sa'id, Faiza's husband, will not bear with a white wife who drinks; Yusuf, the Muslim cleric, will not bear with a wife who celebrates Christmas in the house. Abdirahman, the Muslim cleric in *Offspring of Paradise*, will not accept the idea that a Muslim is the same as a Christian, worse still; he will not substitute water with tissue paper for long call.

In *Offspring of Paradise*, the author lauds cultural fixity as the most appropriate coping strategy to survive overseas. Hana, the heroine, rejects love relationships with Western men and turns to her cultural traditions. She denounces Helen's influence and denigrates the Christian doctrine of salvation. For Abdi, the carrier's world is a destructive one that only leads to failure and so she encourages immigrants to pattern their lives after Abdirahman. She implies that the political strife in Somalia is just but God's retribution for the sins they have committed and that Muslims should avoid the company of non-Muslims particularly at secular hotels. Nonetheless, not all Somali immigrants will embrace fixity as a coping strategy; they are heterogeneous in nature. Has Abdi represented immigrant characters like Mulki who love the company of Tea party ladies? Mulki joins a group of Christian women who share sensitive topics that criticize Somali culture but is not willing to leave it until they disband it on their own. What about Little Hirsi who has partly converted to Christianity to coexist with the dominant group? Abdi seems to suggest that Hirsi is a "desperate failure" unworthy of emulation by all Somali immigrant characters (344). To what extent is this true? To what extent should we blame Hirsi for Helen's criminal tendencies? To what degree should we blame the carriers for Helen's criminal record? What if Hana had been under Rune's tutelage, would she have suffered the misfortune? Just because Hana is unfortunate to be in the hands of a sick carrier does not warrant blanket condemnation of all the carriers. In short, Abdi has attempted to silence immigrant characters with a liking for Western culture, which is a misrepresentation.

Furthermore, Abdi implies that immigrant characters confront ambivalence. The characters vacillate between the two identities. In Spivak's view, the immigrants are heterogeneous and indeed there are those like Sa'id, Usman, and Yusuf in *A Mighty Collision of Two Words* who maintain stable identities. They stick to Islamic traditions and do not waver. In *Offspring of Paradise,* Abdirahman does not fluctuate between hybrid and fixed identities. By emphasizing ambivalence, Abdi attempts to silence those with stable identities, hence misrepresentation.

Pertaining identity, Abdi presents ambivalent identities and fixed identities, some characters fluctuate between Western and African identities, for example, Anisa and Hana. Others like Yusuf, Abdirahman and Sa'id have stable identities. Abdi makes a perfect representation of the migrant identities in the question of identity.

Moreover, the author depicts characters that suffer humiliation in diaspora and return to their mother culture or homeland. Hana abandons Helen and returns to Mulki, Anisa abandons Mike and returns to Rako Island. But to what extent does this apply to the other characters in Abdi's novels given their heterogeneity? Some characters like Little Hirsi in *Offspring of Paradise* are quite happy in the foreign land given that he has secured the material needs of his family by his relationship with the carriers. Hirsi never thinks of returning to his mother culture and motherland. Abdirahman and Yusuf have settled in an American city, spreading the Islamic religion; Yusuf, for instance, converts the white man, Mike to Islam. We do not come across a single incident in the novels where they are humiliated by the host community. Better still, even Anisa's physical return to Rako Island does not change her hybrid identity but just turns her into a transnational migrant who will be going back to the United States with the children to pay their white grandparents visits. By emphasizing abandonment and return, Abdi is silencing those characters who feel at home overseas, hence a misrepresentation.

Abdi also depicts polarity among essentialist groups and how it can lead to political strife in a cosmopolitan society. In *Offspring of Paradise*, she presents to us instances where cultural fixity among Somali clans tatter the social fabric in a nation leading to its total destruction. In *A Mighty Collision of Two Worlds,* polarity between the dominant groups and minority groups in Rako Island is stifled by hybridity thereby evading political strife. Concerning this issue, Abdi takes in consideration heterogeneity in the subaltern, hence perfect representation.

2.4 Conclusion

In this chapter, the role of characters in the depiction of the author's concerns has been analysed. The section has also looked at the manner in which Abdi's concerns are related to themes typical of migration literature and then interrogated Abdi's representation. In the light of the analysis, Abdi has effectively employed characterization to texualize her concerns. Migrant characters like Anisa, Yusuf and Khadija in *A Mighty Collision of Two Worlds* and Hana, Mulki, Abdirahman and Usman in *Offspring of Paradise* effectively convey concerns like coping strategies- hybridity, alienation and fixity; and other concerns such as ambivalence, abandonment and return, identity, cultural conflict and polarity vis-a-vis political strife. In the chapter, Abdi's concerns have been compared with those of migrant literature and similarity established. Migrant literature scholars propose hybridity, ambivalence, identity and abandonment as characteristic themes of literature of migration, all of which are Abdi's concerns. Using Abdi's concerns and characters, Abdi's representation was interrogated and most migrant characters were misrepresented casting a doubt on the capability of migrant authors to speak for the migrant characters abroad.

CHAPTER THREE

Cultural Hybridity and Identity Formation

Introduction

This chapter examines the role of cultural hybridity on the construction of diasporic identity in cosmopolitan societies at home and away. Minorities who dwell in communities with majorities that are very different from them experience similar identity formation challenges like immigrants who join dominant host communities overseas. When African migrant characters reach overseas, they define themselves by the culture of the country of origin but as they interact with the host, white society, they undergo transformation. It does not, however, mean that they abandon their ethnic traditions; the immigrants redefine themselves within the web of existing cultures, their mother culture into the bargain. Ronald Jackson defines identity as "that which confers a sense of personhood. He adds that "it refers to self definition" (9), the attempt to understand who one is. Hylland Eriksen defines identity as "being the same as oneself as well as being different" (60), he therefore suggests that identity does not have to be permanent; the immigrant can retain his or her ethnic identity (being oneself) and adopt foreign habits (being different), which is the essence of cultural hybridity. While defining cultural hybridity, Thomas Elliot writes:

> Modern migration has transplanted a mixture of social, religious, economic or political determinations and migrants have taken

> with them only one part of the original culture and the new culture […], what has developed on the new soil is bafflingly both alike and different from the parent culture. Moreover, in such situation, culture sympathy and culture clash emerge. (63-64)

Elliot's 'half' culture is the connecting ligament between cultures in a cosmopolitan world; it is what Bhabha refers to as the "in-between" space that stands both "different and alike" at the same time (54). Kalva Virinder et al define hybridity as a "process of cultural mixing in which immigrants adopt the aspects of the host culture and rework, reform and reconfigure them in production of new hybrid culture or hybrid identities" (71). It therefore follows that identity construction among immigrants cannot be detached from cultural hybridity given the diverse cultures the immigrants confront in the diaspora. The new culture alters the immigrants' self identification as they start negotiating their existence in the new environment. Jacomijne Prins et al observe that "identities are constructed and negotiated through interaction" (81), which therefore means that the immigrants' identities change when they encounter societies that are completely different from their culture of origin. Nonetheless, as aforementioned, the identity change brought by hybridity is not a permanent change; it is rather fluid and flexible. H. Zubida et al assert that identity formation among immigrants is "a continuous process in which the host country and origin country or neither of them creates dynamic patterns of identity" (2). They define cultural hybridity as "multiplicity, dynamicity and flexibility of the identity formation process" among immigrants. They postulate that immigrants can hold contradicting identities with loose boundaries, which is a reference to Bhabha's "in-betweenness"; a space where the immigrant is not "this or that" but is rather "both this and that" and neither "this and that" (227), the circumstances in which a number of migrant characters in Abdi's novels find themselves in. They are not "Somali or white" but rather both "Somali and white" and neither "Somali nor white". The chapter looks at identity as a changeable construct, a process of "becoming" rather than "being" as Abdi's characters negotiate their existence overseas.

The principal characters in this chapter are Hana, Helen, Usman, Mulki, Khadra's daughter, Zahra and Siraat in *Offspring of Paradise* and Anisa, Sa'id, Omar, Mike, the personal secretary, Usman, Yusuf and Khadija in *A Mighty Collision of Two Worlds*. Hana is the heroine in *Offspring of Paradise*, a second generation immigrant who arrives in a British city at a tender age of eight years with her frail grandmother fleeing political strife in Somalia. Helen is a white woman who works for a Christian evangelical organization in the refugee camp. The evangelical organization calls itself the carriers, which means "the carriers of the good news "or "the gospel". They befriend Muslim youth to convert them to Christianity, and that is why Helen becomes Hana's "best friend". Usman is a former confidante of Helen's who got expelled from school as a result of absenteeism caused by their friendship. He trails Helen and Hana to dissuade young immigrants like Hana to shun her company in order to acquire formal education and uphold their religion. Khadra's daughter is a child to Abdirahman and Khadra, immigrants who arrived overseas in their adulthood. Abdirahman is a Muslim cleric who takes advantage of the constitutional space the immigrant is given by the foreign state to teach young immigrants their language and religion. Mulki is Hana's guardian in the diaspora. She hails from the marginalized clan that overthrows the government of Somalia and persecutes the ruling clan, which happens to be Hana's clan. Mulki is a university student at Mogadishu when Somalia plunges in political strife and so she arrives at the wall (refugee camp) in her early twenties. Her good education background enables her to secure a job with the wall's administration as the interpreter. Zahra is Mulki's colleague at the university but hails from the ruling clan, which is persecuted by Mulki's clan. After the demise of her parents, she seeks refuge at Mulki's home but Mulki's father's efforts to rescue her are hampered by many militias on the escape route. They leave her somewhere to assess the security of the route but when they return, they do not find her. Siraat is an immigrant who works alongside Abdirahman in teaching young Somali Muslim immigrants their language and religion. Anisa is the heroine in *A Mighty Collision of Two Worlds*. She leaves for the United States on a school exchange program during her puberty but takes advantage of the scholarship to acquire formal education in the US city. Sa'id is a committed Muslim at Rako Island, the imaginary setting of *A Mighty Collision of Two Worlds* in the East. He is so dedicated to Islam that he starts an organization to persuade non-Muslims to be converted to Islam. He is the husband to a character called Faiza, Anisa's neighbour. Usman is Sa'id's friend who works closely with him to spread a radical brand of Islam at Rako Island; they are arrested and detained together. The personal secretary is a Muslim who works closely with the secular government at Rako Island till the president appoints him as his personal secretary. He is despised by fellow Muslims but they turn to him for help when Sa'id and Usman are detained on framed charges. Omar is Anisa's uncle who inherits Anisa's mother, Halima, and brings Anisa up after her father's demise. Mike is the white young man who falls in love with Anisa in the United States and marries her. As a result, he converts to Islam and relocates to Rako Island. Yusuf and Khadija are Somali couple in the United States. Yusuf is a Muslim cleric, who runs an Islamic centre to strengthen Islamic faith overseas. He oversees Mike's conversion to Islam and his wife gives Anisa moral support when she becomes sick.

In this chapter, cultural hybridity in Abdi's fiction is negotiated in terms of narrative stories about construction of identity in the diaspora which may depict hybrid identities in terms of cultural encounter in Western cities. The chapter will explore the impact of Western culture on the migrant characters' identity. It will then analyse hybrid identities in Abdi's fiction by investigating whether Somali immigrants in Western cities create a middle ground where they stand between Somali culture and Western culture. The chapter will also find out whether the middle ground results in inner conflicts within migrant characters and how it affects identity construction in the foreign country. The chapter will then close by examining the relationship between hybrid characters with the dominant group in Abdi's fiction.

3.1 The Impact of Western Culture on the Characters' Identity

> Identity is not bound only by origin; rather it is social context and has its effect on one's psyche and desire. Identity is structured through time and is associated with the economic situation that one lives in and the position of the self in different cultural contexts. One's origin is the reality that cannot be changed and has its place and roots within the self but the society that one lives in has a great influence on the self. However, people are free to choose which identity they have but this does not prevent some variations in the new identity as a result of other cultural meanings and symbols. (Sulyman, 20)

Areen Sulyman, in the above citation reiterates the assertion that identity is a process that is subject to the prevailing cultural and economic conditions. Abdi's characters arrive in Western cities with a Somali-Islamic identification, but the Western society they live in influences them to become somewhat different. When Anisa Ali, in *A Mighty Collision of Two Worlds,* arrives in the United States as student on scholarship, she is a *fixed* character in that she fanatically holds on her Islamic religion. Her white American roommate, Florence, abridged as Floor, describes Anisa as "some sort of freak" (41), by reason of her habitual prayers. Anisa reads from her mother's script with utmost zeal that *salat* (prayer) is "the connection between the created and the Creator" (33), and it is unthinkable for a Muslim to miss it. Anisa therefore resolves to stick to her ethnic traditions, which is the spine of cultural fixity.

As essentialising as cultural fixity is, she realizes that she is very different from Americans. First, she discovers that American girls are materialistic as opposed to simple, frugal Somali girls; she looks at Florence's possessions in utter shock, for example, Florence unpacks "layers upon layers of shirts, T-shirts, jeans, pants, underclothes and shoes" (40); there are also albums, loose photos, and a year's ration of sweets, chewing gum, cookies and potato chips. Unlike Anisa who carries the Holy Quran, Florence carries books and novels. Her little possessions are no match for Florence's hence elevating cultural difference. As time elapses, Anisa singles out more differences as she interacts with American girls at Fairwood. Unlike Muslim girls at Rako Isand, American girls start romantic affairs with boys very early, her friend Floor is no exception. In fact, when Anisa tells Florence that she does not "see boys around"; Florence retorts that Anisa is socially "dumb" (40). It astonishes her further to learn that the girls steal each other's boyfriends. Lisa is a case in point, she steals Floor's boyfriend; it confounds Anisa further to learn that in the United States, some women commit suicide when lovers jilt them. Lisa's mother is one such an example. The individualism in Floor's nature also magnifies the difference between her Eastern heritage and their Western heritage. Whereas at Rako Island all Muslims are family, in Floor's opinion, it is "archaic" and outdated to take a life style in which everyone is a relative. She says, "I can't endorse such social network, it is archaic, don't you think?" (44). In the ensuing conversation with Floor, Anisa takes note of the weak marriage institutions in America. Floor's mother divorces the father, abandons the children, moves in with another man and her father resorts to cohabiting with another woman. This marriage breakage has a negative psychological effect on Florence who smokes as a kind of escapism from the painful realities. To Anisa, smoking is an uncommon vice among Muslim girls at Rako Island and it underscores the difference further.

Going by these differences, Anisa creates what we can refer to as American/Rakon duality, two factions in binary opposition: materialistic/frugal, immoral/chaste, individualistic/communalistic and weak marriages/strong marriages respectively. At this point, Anisa interprets her identity experience as being more attached to the ethnic culture in spite of living in the United States. Her identification is related to the ethnic group, Somali culture, although the environment around her is American. Jaspal and Cinnirella argue that "identification of people with their ethnic group has its positive embodiment for the belonging principles of identity" (510). The immigrants are respected overseas if they can differentiate themselves from others, and so Anisa's choice of difference enables her to locate herself in the cosmopolitan city. Nonetheless, as earlier mentioned identity is a changeable or mobile construct and should be regarded in terms of "becoming" rather than "being", and so Anisa's cultural identity has just begun the process of hybridisation.

Anisa interacts with the white society and starts imbibing Western values consciously and unconsciously. Although her friends had got used to her patterns of life, she still altered herself. Abdi writes: "Anisa was also fast learning more and more about the host country. Slowly but surely, she was also beginning to understand and sometimes even beginning to adopt albeit unconsciously, some of the mannerisms and habits of her girlfriends," (48). The environment gradually transforms Anisa, even without her conscious desire to adopt some of these aspects, and her age complicates the matter even more. Like Waiyaki in Ngugi Wa Thiong'o's *The River Between,* it is almost impossible for the mere pubescent she is to confront Western influence successfully in a white dominated environment. Anisa starts losing piety by skipping prayers because of the unconscious belief that Americans cannot pray like people at Rako Island since they have a lot to do. And when she prays, the narrator observes that "she prays very fast like a thief for fear of being seen by the others," (49), and worse still adopts Western character attributes like individualism. She no longer joins fellow Muslims for prayer and arguing that "her prayers and social life were things that concerned only her" (54). At this point, she is becoming similar to Floor, even echoing Floor's earlier views about communal nature of her people at Rako Island. She also loses her chastity by taking an American boyfriend, Mike Paterson, and visiting social places, while consoling herself that everyone is doing it. She says, "[t]he crux of the matter is that she wasn't alone in her fascination with the exciting individualistic lifestyle. Everyone enjoyed life on the fast track, and loud and riotous music had an appeal of its own," (54).

Although initially everything about the West was scandalous, she starts to see Western aspects in a positive manner: her liking for Western culture is palpable. She discards some of her ethnic morals to integrate in the white dominated alien community. Of Mike Paterson, an irreligious white young man, she observes that "he is very persevering and not pushy" (59). Anisa gives him Islamic literature and since he loves her, Mike starts studying them to acquaint himself with his girlfriend's way of life. Apparently, Anisa's hybridisation has just begun.

Before she returns to Rako Island on vacation, Florence remarks that she is "cute" and "kind of exotic" (59), to refer to the change Anisa has undergone. Anisa's self has gradually transited from cultural fixity (ethnic identity) to identity construction process that will enable her to coexist with the dominant group. Back at Rako Island, her friend Faiza is surprised when she mentions her fiancé's name; it is queer to entertain a love relationship between Anisa Ali and Mike Paterson in Rako Island. Her relatives are desirous to see her get married to the state secretary's son, Sayid Jibreel but when he comes to woo her; Anisa displays the assertiveness typical of the American woman and cannot be compatible with the conservative (fixed) Sayid. She confesses that if there is a quality she has picked in the United States then it is "to declare a simple NO" (81). She exhibits open contempt at fixed or rather conservative characters, for instance, she wonders how Faiza's fiancé, Sa'id, can visit the West and come back not having heard "Michael Jackson's latest album or set foot in a disco joint" (84). She therefore approves adoption of Western values like clubbing or rather reveling, which is prohibited in the Islamic tradition. She rejects her arranged marriage to the secretary's son, which echoes Floor's remarks in their first conversation at Fairwood. Floor had discredited Anisa's community's arrangement to have Anisa's uncle, Omar, inherit her mother but now it is Anisa that scoffs at her community's arrangement to have her married. She candidly tells Sayid Jibreel that "a wife is no cook" when he makes snide remarks about the cup of tea she had prepared for him: "[i]f it is a lady cook you are looking for, Sayid Jibreel, you won't find her here! So how about taking your troubles to some other door?" (91). Anisa would not have made such a remark when she first arrived abroad; it is a feminist remark acquired in the West. Faiza's effort to defend Jibreel comes in conflict with her determined opposition. She contends that black people are not "monopolies of truth" and given chance, Mike can be "a better Muslim than Faiza" (95). During this process of "becoming", Anisa now loves and appreciates Mike, with his race. She drops the *hijab* and when uncle Omar reminds her that her father was very pious, she retorts that her father and she only resemble in body. Her mind has aspects of Western thinking; just as Floor takes care of herself so can Anisa "perfectly take care of herself" (97). Later on, after marriage to Mike, she paves way to breaking the marriage, another Western attribute she had previously condemned.

In *Offspring of Paradise,* Hana flees with her grandmother to a European city owing to political upheavals in Somalia. Her father is assassinated and her mother's whereabouts unknown, she is a migrant at the age of eight years. Her only surviving relative is the hoary grandmother who arrives abroad with forged documents, a crime severely punishable in the host nation. Since Rune, the senior administrator of the refugee camp, works for a Christian organisation that convert young Muslims to Christianity, he ignores the old lady's forgery and hands them to Mulki, a Somali interpreter, to look after them. The refugee camp, otherwise referred to as *the Wall,* accommodates many Somali immigrants. Siraat teaches her to read and write Somali, an attempt to give her ethnic identity and Abdirahman teaches her Somali language and to memorize the Quran. Having attained her ethnic identity, the European government directs that all immigrant children should have formal, Western education. Hana joins elementary school, which is a cosmopolitan class and she starts noticing the cultural difference. A white classmate calls her 'dark skull' (76), and Hana vents her anger by kicking a chair till one of its legs breaks; the episode signifies the birth of cultural fixity in Hana's life. Her grandmother's presence by her side represents the Somali heritage and identity. Hana prevails upon the grandmother, to narrate her history, which is an effort to understand her ethnic identity via what Hall refers to as "passionate research" for the "organic community" (393). She insists on "knowing everything" (88) about her past, which compels her grandmother to tell her the story of her father's assassination, the destruction of Mogadishu and leaves other details on a tape. Apart from realizing that she has a heritage of strife, death and despair, she understands the polarity among Somali clans. After her grandmother's death, Hana shuns Mulki's surrogate parenting not just because she comes from the militia clan but because during their flight from Somalia, she abandoned Zahra, in the wilderness and was never found. Mulki's attempts to explain the difficulty of fleeing with a woman branded *fagash* (loyalist) out of Mogadishu falls on her deaf ears. Hana assumes a fixed identity and denounces Mulki, sayings, "[y]our friend Zahra, she trusted you, but what did you do? You dumped her!" (104).

At this juncture, Hana has assigned herself an identity based on a common ancestry with other Somali people. It is the ethnic identity that as Jaspal and Cinnirella observes "gives positive embodiment for the belonging principles of identity" (510). In other words, like Anisa, it gives Hana a positive implication about her identity to be in position to differentiate herself from others overseas. However, Hana's hybridisation has just begun since the identity of the immigrant is a process of "becoming" as opposed to "being". Oblivious of fluidity of hybridisation, Hana gets so obsessed with her ethnic identity (cultural fixity) that she attacks Mulki for failing to protect Zahra. And since Mulki could not "be trusted with Zahra's life", Hana is not prepared to entrust her with her own life. She rides roughshod over Mulki and forges a relationship with Helen Banister, a white *carrier* member. Whereas in *A Mighty Collision of Two Worlds* hybridisation process stems from love and sex, the shift in *Offspring of Paradise* stems from polarity within the Somali Society. There is perpetual struggle between the dominant and minority clans, after which the latter subverts the authority of the dominant clan. The polarity is replayed overseas where Hana subverts Mulki's authority. Fanon, however, gives this subversion another cause; in his work *Black Skin, White Masks,* he notes that "every neurosis, every abnormal manifestation is a product of a cultural situation". He writes, "[t]here is a constellation of postulates, a series of propositions that slowly and subtly- with help of books, newspapers, films, radio- work their way into one's mind and shape their view of the world of the group to which he belongs," (152).

The constant pictures of dying Somalis that Hana has watched on television abroad have greatly contributed to Hana's negative perception of the Somali people. Commenting on the Somali woman who symbolizes the Somali society, Abdi writes, "Hana knows her from TV; the darling of the candid camera. The daily bread of the news hounds, for she is what makes news, the very spirit of human tragedy. The picture has followed Hana to *the wall,"* (95). The domination of Western ways of thinking has created a world that stifles Mulki's lone black voice as Hana climbs the stave into the white society. She has repressed her African voice and grand mother's voice but not eradicated it as Fanon observes. It is just awaiting an opportune moment to stand out, fight back and result in a severe psychological trauma.

Hana meets Helen after school and when Mulki demands to know where she has been, she blurts, "[w]as having lunch with Helen" (100). Helen eagerly accepts and appreciates her friendship and their relationship starts with a bang. As she interacts with the dominant group, Hana unconsciously starts acquiring new habits, for example, Mulki realizes that she does not apply the Somali recipe when cooking tea. She "dumps lipton tea bag in each mug, throws cardamom in it and sets on the microwave," (109). Hana cycles to school, which is not in league with the Somali tradition; cycling, according to Somali culture, is dishonorable for the girl, it is a reserve for men from humble families. The *carriers,* a Christian cult, open their arms to receive her though with strings attached; they are an organized group of influential people with a systematic strategy to convert African Muslim youth to their brand of Christianity. Taking advantage of the search for her mother, they lead Hana by the nose into the church. Even when Rune proffers his hand for greeting, Hana shakes it at the expense of Islamic traditions. She has appreciated their company such that she can no longer obey Islamic rules, which stipulate complete separation of sexes. She is clad in "blue trousers, blue winter jacket with long braided hair hanging limply on each side of her shoulders" (162), which is a transgression of the Islamic code of dress. Hana does not wear a scarf as Muslim girls should, yet another contravention of the Islamic tradition she subscribes to. Hana has also acquired a kind of independence that Khadra's daughter envies, independence typical of American girls.

Khadra's daughter envies her freedom because as a second generation immigrant, she grows up with Western culture and does not find any problem with it. She observes Hana "pop in and depart anytime she likes" (222), like other American girls. American culture inculcates individuality and individualism among students; it denigrates the communal Islamic culture. Hana tells Usman that even if Helen derails her from her Islamic faith, "it is up to her, and not anyone else" (229). Hana unconsciously acquires Western values from the foreign environment. Despite remaining a Muslim, her close interaction with Rune, Jason, Helen and other *carriers* has a great impact on her. Had Helen not messed up the plan, with her haste, Hana would have been fully assimilated.

3.2 Hybrid Identities in Abdi's Fiction

Migrant characters in Abdi's narratives create a cultural hybridity in the construction of their identities at three major levels: the *shared sense*, the *in-between* and the *more ethnic* hybrid identities. The three hybrid identities reject the *us/them* binary opposition that is typical of ethnic or fixed identities.

3.2:1 Shared Sense Hybrid Identities

In Abdi's *A Mighty Collision of Two Worlds*, there are characters whose identities have been shaped by the new culture such that they appreciate both their ethnic culture and foreign values in an equal measure. Anisa, the heroine of the novel, is brought up by her uncle, Omar after her father's demise. They live in Rako Island which has a dominant Christian majority and a Muslim minority. Uncle Omar's experience with Christian and secular majority at the Island has inculcated in him tolerance with other communities. He exhibits a *shared sense* of cultural hybridity where a member of the minority group takes half of each culture in the cosmopolitan environment. In his research on construction of identity among Kurdish immigrants in Sweden, Sulyman depicts *shared sense* hybridity via an immigrant called Aram. In an interview, Aram says:

> I came to Sweden when I was twenty-two years and I have lived here for fifteen years. At the beginning, I felt I was still in my country (Iraq Kurdistan) but after five to six years, I integrated very successfully in the society. At that time, I had changed a little bit and found myself fifty percent each. I could not see myself as Swede or Kurd. However, after six years, I tried to change because the more one integrates in a society of another culture; the more one learns their habit from a particular perspective and cannot be part from it. But after a period of time, I did know that I am not Swedish in my face but some of their ideas have become part of my life. Therefore I can say that I have two identities, the first one is Kurdish and the second is Swedish. (28)

Like Aram in Sweden, Uncle Omar is aware that he is neither a Christian nor an atheist like the majority in Rako Island but some of their ideas have become part of his life. He has learnt, from the culture of Rako Island the importance of formal education and takes Anisa to a Christian Catholic Mission School: St Joseph. He has also learnt that formal education when acquired abroad has many benefits; he knows that in Rako Island, "going to the United states is every kid's dream"

(26), and that is the reason he opposes Anisa's mother and allows Anisa to leave for Fairwood, USA, saying, "it'd be an enriching experience" (30). Furthermore, Omar has seen the people of Rako Island interact with white tourists and their girls have married white people, and that is why Anisa's marriage relationship does not stun him. After receiving a letter from his white son-in law, Mike Paterson, to inform him of his marriage to Anisa, Omar points out the positive side of Mike. He asserts that he loves his frankness and sincerity, "[t]his man is straight to the point, a very truthful man" (150). He adds that few Muslims would be as honest as Mike is, especially about his spiritual condition. When Anisa's mother dismisses his assertions, Omar asks him to contrast between Mike who can reveal their marriage to them with Anisa, the Muslim, who marries an atheist and goes underground. He suggests that Anisa, the practising Muslim is hypocritical as juxtaposed to Mike, the atheist, who tells his honest truth. Mike abducts the children after the separation and flees to the United States of America, and few years later, Anisa proposes dissolution of the marriage in spite of her earlier criticism of the weak marriage institutions in the United States.

Nevertheless, Uncle Omar defends Mike contending that like any other "son of Adam, he deserves fair treatment too" (310). Better still, he insists that Mike has a right to be involved in the dissolution of the marriage. For this reason, Uncle Omar directs Anisa to write to Mike, insisting that he is human, hence the need for dialogue. When Anisa argues that Mike was neither a Muslim nor married to her, Uncle Omar dismisses her extremities and demands to know how certain she is about her assertions. "[i]f you aren't married to him, how can we neutralize a marriage that doesn't exist?" (307). He adds that Mike is a promising Muslim who is making progress Anisa's imposition of the religion notwithstanding. Omar's appreciation of a man not of his race is a sterling depiction of his *shared sense* hybridity. It is his ability to accept the whites that lays a strong foundation to the mixed marriage between Anisa and Mike. Mike observes later that although Anisa and Omar are related, their traits "differ like the east and west" (450). He says this because of Anisa's reversion to cultural fixity later in the story. In spite of his white race, Mike exhibits a *shared sense* hybridity in *A Mighty Collision of Two Worlds*. Although he is white, he falls in love and marries a Somali Muslim girl and then converts to Islam, joining the minority Muslims in a white Christian majority. He takes a new name, Ali Ahmed Patterson and is subsequently discriminated against by the secular and Christian majority. Before conversion to Islam, Mike detests perverts just as the Muslims do, Anisa tells Yusuf, "Mike, he can't just be bothered to feel chummy with perverts," (138). After conversion, he reads Islamic books in the library; Yusuf gives him a blue cover book which he reads thoroughly from cover to cover. He adopts new practices that Islam prescribes as handed down by his wife Anisa, for instance, "brushing teeth before breakfast, using water to wash after long call and taking food by the left hand" (164). When they visit Rako Island, Mike attends all his prayers, and the first rate at which he learns the religion impresses the Muslim community at Rako Island till they approve Anisa's choice of spouse.

On their return to the United States of America, Anisa reverts to ethnic identity (fixity), which kindles a hostile reaction from Mike's relatives. Mike's mother denounces his wife and criticizes the Islamic religion but Mike maintains his cool for he neither distastes his mother nor his wife. The two symbolize two contending cultures, the West and the East in a binary opposition. Mike enters the middle ground where he has the partial culture that is both "different" and "alike" simultaneously (Elliot, 63-64). The East, which begged to stay is invading, adulterating and taking over the Western space. This explains Mike's mother's declaration that Christianity is "a badge of honour of the white tradition and she was not about to bow to some black alien daughter" (178). There are those members of the white community who call Anisa 'a black thing' before Mike's face and he candidly tells them that "the black thing is his wife". Elliot refers to this as "culture sympathy and culture clash" (63-64), that result from cultural hybridity. Whereas Mike sympathises with Eastern culture, her mother detests it, so he negotiates existence between "his wife's taxing rules and society's scoffs at the rules" (179), and continues to love his family.

The Muslim spokesman who also is the president's personal secretary at Rako Island demonstrates *shared sense* hybrid identity. The Kurdish immigrant Aram observes that "the more integrates, the more one learns the habits of a certain culture and cannot be apart from it" (28), and indeed in spite of hailing from the minority community in Rako Island, he has worked his way up the social ladder by forging friendly relations with Christians and atheists. The secular president, who recognizes his Islamic identity, trusts him such that he has appointed him as his personal secretary. When the Muslim radicals like Sa'id are detained on trumped charges of drug peddling, the personal secretary is in the appropriate position to negotiate their release and the president sets them free. He succeeds where many others have failed because he has forged strong relationships with the dominant secular majority at Rako.

Mohamed and Nasra, Mike's children, love both the African mother and white American father. When their mother flees with them to Rako Island, they miss their father so much that whenever they spot a white man in glasses, they come back elated and tell their mother that they have seen their father, Mike. When their father kidnaps and takes them to the United States, they miss their mother, Anisa so much that it compels Mike to come back to Rako Island. Like Aram, they are fifty percent Somali and Fifty percent White, which signifies double identity typical of shared sense hybrid identity. The white relatives abridge Mohamed's name to MED, to represent the third space where the East and the West negotiate into a new identity. Irritated by the change, Anisa says: "[s]ix months out of my sight and Mohamed's name is cut into three parts and the poor boy is made to walk away with only a third so as to make his grandmother happy. What a shame (485)". The three parts Anisa refers to is the third space where Mohammed starts to exasperate her mother who by now has taken to cultural fixity as a coping strategy.

3.2:2 The In-between Hybrid Identities

There are characters who vacillate between the culture of host community and that of their countries of origin in Abdi's narratives. While investigating ambivalence among adolescent immigrants in the diaspora, Zubida et al remark that immigrant children face conflicting social contexts in which they attempt to incorporate "here" and "there" into meaningful sense of the "self". Alejandro Portes and Rumbaut Rubiin write:

> Among adolescent immigrants, this process is more complex and often entails the juggling of competing allegiances and attachments. Situated within two cultural worlds, they must define themselves in relation to multiple reference groups (sometimes in two countries and languages) and the

classifications in which they are placed by their native peers, schools, the ethnic community and larger society. (304)

Hana and Anisa reach the Western cities in their adolescent period, a time when they are forming their personal identities and confront rival cultures in the cosmopolitan environment. As they struggle with their identity crises, during puberty, they must also define themselves in relation to the multiple cultures around them; consequently, they end up with contradicting identities with loose boundaries. Bhabha refers to these identities as "in-between" identities, defined as identities in which humans are not "this or that" but are both "this or that" and neither "this and that". He stresses that hybridity is "a constant state of contestation and flux caused by differential systems [...] the unstable element of linkage" (227).

It is quite difficult to predict Hana and Anisa's positions on the identity continuum; at one point they exhibit *more ethnic* hybrid identity, other times *shared sense* hybrid identity and yet other times *Western skewed* hybrid identity. When she arrives in the United States, she sticks to her Islamic traditions: prays five times a day well aware that *salat* is "the connection between the Creator and the creature" (Abdi, *A Mighty Collision of Two Worlds*, 33), she is not materialistic and it does not surprise her when Floor remarks that "she has so little herself" (39), Anisa loves the arranged marriages, polygamy marriages, including widow inheritance in her culture and defends it against Floor's criticism. She says that "a man can have more than one wife [...] it is preferable to mistresses, family break ups, child neglect and child neglect" (42), common in the West. Although she had earlier on detested polygamy, Anisa "sees the wisdom of it after the death of her father" (43), insisting that it ensures the security of the orphans.

Her tendency to refer to the Islamic religion to back up her arguments with Floor proves that she is of the *more ethnic* hybrid identity: a devout Somali Muslim in a Western, secular environment. She tells Floor that "Muslims are bound by Allah to help the helpless, the old and the orphans" (43), to depict her unwavering dedication to her culture. However, as the story unfolds, Anisa's conduct proves that she is not the conservative Somali we have just witnessed. The narrator says that "her letters" became "less and less detailed about her nonexistent spiritual life" (53). Anisa loves the West, her "uncle's pleas to return home for holidays fell on deaf ears" (53). She spends her leisure times with "friends at discos" and the *Isha* prayers of her high school days had become a thing of the past" (54), by reason of the Western individualism that eats into her Somali soul. At this point, Anisa is neither Somali nor white, neither Christian nor Muslim; she is entering the ambivalent site, the in-between space.

Her reasons for not praying is given as: "[s]he still respected her folks, but she had come to believe that her prayers and social life were now things that concerned only her," (54).The individualism she alludes to here is a salient feature of Western culture, which is inconsistent to the communalism she defended earlier on when she was a *more ethnic* hybrid. Anisa's love affair with Mike is another sign of her shifting identity. They date many times, meeting at nightclubs and disco joints, stifling the ethnic identity by arguing that she was not the only one making the shift towards integration: "[a]nd she was consoled by the fact that they were also no different from her. Like her, they went to the nightspots and disco joints. So brazen were they in their ways and mode of speech that you couldn't set them apart from their hosts," (54). In speech, Anisa now twangs like the white hosts and she cannot be distinguished from them; she has moved far away from what can be specifically described as *more Somali hybrid* identity and stands at the *Western skewed hybrid* stave. But as earlier emphasized, identity is flexible and unstable at the in-between space and being at this space Anisa is in a constant state of "becoming"; she is neither "this nor that". When Mike proposes marriage, she blurts: "You are Kafir, Mike, that's what is wrong- nothing that we can see in the water" (65). Anisa has now shifted from the *Western skewed* hybrid identity to the *more Somali* hybrid identity. It is astounding and heart chilling for Mike who has loved her so much this long as she adds more aspersions that magnify the difference:

> My dear Mike, let's quit pretending. You are an unbeliever and you are very much aware of your condition. It isn't as if you didn't know your *kufr*. You know you are unbeliever and there is nothing you relish more than the state you are in. and so does everyone else know. (65)

Anisa cannot recall that she has also participated in Mike's heathen life style: dancing at discos together, taking wine together, not reciting the Quran together, not fasting and not praying together. In the ensuing conversation, Anisa talks to him about Islamic traditions like prayer: "people must be doing *maghrib*," she says, and adds that Muslims should pray five times a day. Mike says he has never found her doing it. But she insists, "[w]e are supposed to pray to the Almighty five times a day" (69), she blurts, almost raising her voice. When Mike replies that he may never understand her prayers, Anisa breaks down and cries. The in-between hybrid identity shifts her mind from one identity to another on the identity continuum thereby causing a struggle within her. She now is at the middle ground where she is not Somali, not white but is partially Somali and partially white as opposed to Mike who by has *shared sense* hybrid with both white and Somali.

Barzoo Elliasi observes that "immigrants' modes of belonging are often questioned and challenged by dominant subjects because they experience the problem of where they belong and not knowing where one belongs" (53), and so is Anisa's case; at the middle ground, she does not know where she belongs. Her identity construction process is on and as James Clifford puts it, immigrants (such as Anisa) "construct identities outside the national time and space in order to live inside" (251). They are the belated citizens who try to catch up with the rest of the indigenous citizens albeit with a baggage of traditions from the country of origin yet determined to fit in the nation. The construction of the migrant's identity is therefore a painful process and it is worse when the immigrant does not understand the "self". Anisa is one such immigrant that does not understand the self; she is not aware of what she is experiencing. When Mike asks her why she is crying, she replies, "[i]t's nothing, [...] could be I am coming down with flu" (69). She is not aware that her hybrid identity under the process of construction and her psychological trauma is bound to escalate. Peter Burke and Jan Stets emphasize that "the relationship between the 'self' and identity is crucial because self influences society through actions and society influences self through shared language and meanings that enable the person to take the role of the other" (128). Consequently, Anisa (self) is acting on the society (by relating with Mike) and she has to understand "the self" (herself) to understand society (Mike). When she returns to Rako Island on vacation, Anisa turns into a defender of Western culture from all the criticism by her friends and relatives. Her friend Faiza exclaims at Mike's picture saying it is "chalk white" (79), Anisa retorts, "and pinky-cream, silly, there is blood in those veins" (79).

When Faiza insinuates that Mike worships dogs, Anisa replies that "he is allergic to dogs" (80), she criticizes Sa'id, Faiza's husband for visiting a Western city without deigning to step in a disco joint and listen to Michael Jackson's latest album. She says that it proves "his lack of style" (84), and to this category, she adds Sayid Jibreel, the suitor her parents have chosen to marry her. Anisa bluntly tells him that she has come to Rako Island for vacation and she can find a suitor without the "matchmaking of your aunts" (92), hence choosing Mike instead of him. Faiza's attempts to put in some good words for Jibreel meet her resistance; Faiza's defense is based on identity question: as a Muslim, Jibreel will wake Anisa up for prayers, but "Mr. Paterson can't forsake his bed for the sake of the spirit" (96). Faiza cannot understand Anisa's identity situation; she has now shifted to the *Western skewed* hybrid identity where the West is the favourite culture.

While disputing fixity among immigrants, Frederic Cooper and Rogers Brubaker define identity as "one's sense of who one is, of one's social location and of how one is prepared to act" (17). Anisa is prepared to reject Somali culture in this social situation basing on the values she has acquired in the West in the recent past. She understands herself from the Western perspective and locates herself differently in spite of having exhibited ethnic identities in a recent past. She blurts, "[g]ive me a break, I can perfectly take care of myself," (97), and immediately develops an acute migraine, a symptom of the inner conflict resulting from her identity split. The Anisa who a few weeks before criticizes Mike as a heathen now defends him before Faiza to the extent that she crowns him better Muslim than both Faiza and Sayid Jibreel. She says, "Mike will embrace Islam and might even become a better Muslim than you Faiza," (95), and upon return to America, she weds him in a civil marriage.

After Mike's and Anisa's wedding, the reader expects Anisa's identity instability to come to an end, assuming that she has fully integrated into the white society. But one evening, Anisa demands that Mike converts to Islam in a manner that reveals a lot of agony and inner turmoil. "There is every reason to hurry things up. You promised" (116) and she weeps. Anisa asserts that she is not married because they have not had an Islamic wedding. She has now abandoned the *Western skewed* hybrid identity and reverted to the *more ethnic* hybrid identity, and the two contradict each other. Mike is shocked when she tells him that she suffers "the uncomfortable feeling of living in sin" (117), and she follows it with weeping, to reveal her inner conflict. Her ethnic identity reasserts itself and from now up to the moment she flees back to Rako Island, Anisa exhibits the *more ethnic-Somali* hybrid identity. She tells Mike that he "must be crazy to think that the feelings she has for him can be compared to the love she has for her "Maker and my beloved prophet" (119). Although Anisa now believes that she has restored her ethnic identity, we are aware of her double identity; when Mike returns to the Island towards the end of the story; she welcomes him and promises to live with him as he is. They in fact wed afresh and she says it is time "for friendship and they will not be suspicious of each other" (464).

In *Offspring of Paradise,* there are migrant characters who vacillate at the ambivalent space to negotiate their existence in Western cities. Hana, the heroine of the story, is one of these characters who faces "conflicting social contexts" and attempts to "incorporate "here" and "there" into meaningful sense of "self" (Erickson, 220). In his research on Kurdish immigrants in Sweden, Sulyman comes across a Kurdish immigrant, Shilan, who having migrated to Sweden at six months sometimes feels "full Kurd" and other times "in-between" and other times just "different". She says:

> There is a difference when you are between them, in which many things are said and happen that makes you feel a stranger. I always identify and consider myself a Kurd when I think of myself personally and never considered myself for a moment as a Swede and I do not know the reason. However, there are things that might make me look like them, and I have learnt from them because of the society and environment surrounding me. I can say I am a Kurd but not like those Kurds in Kurdistan. It is like in-between. I feel "full Kurd" at home but when I am outside, I have some Swedish culture upon me. (28-29)

At least Shilan feels "full Kurd" at home; on the contrary, Hana becomes a stranger at home, after her grandmother's demise. Hana rejects Mulki's surrogate parenting accusing her of having been responsible for Zahra's death. Nonetheless, like Shilan, Hana sees herself as "full Somali" and Muslim; Rune tells Helen that despite losing everything, she always rushes home to fulfill *salat* (prayer) as a pillar of Islam. Rune says, "[h]er religion is about the only thing that she's got left" (207); this is a proof of her firm attachment to her cultural heritage and alterations she has made on her identity. Hana attends a Christian mass at school and when the priest gives her sacrament, she "immediately spat the wetted stuff into a paper napkin" (150), to signify a rejection of Christianity. Ironically, she resents Mulki and casts aspersions at fellow Somali migrant characters, the very people she claims to identify with. Mulki warns her against keeping Helen's company but she retorts that she should mind her business.

Hana rejects Usman's advice when he warns her against keeping Helen's company; she says, "[a]t the end of the day, it is really upto me and not to anyone else. And prayer never hurt anyone. But guns do. So goodbye" (229). Apparently, Hana deserts the *more ethnic* hybrid identity and stands at the *Western skewed* hybrid position. Hana's relationship with her fellow Somalis can be described as suspicious, sarcastic and hostile, for example, she tells Usman, "the kind of brother we could all depend on. Bravo Somali brother! Where was your bravery when your brothers dumped me here in the cold! Brave man!" (230). Of Abdirahman, her Quranic teacher, she says that "he too is a man, a Somali man so he too must share in the punishment," (233). She even goes a step farther to vouch that she would never let a Somali man to know her mother's whereabouts. She does not mind that Helen, the Christian *carrier* knows where her mother is.

Hana keeps a diary in which she records things in her own version, she asserts that she does not record things the Somali way, "[n]ot in a Somali women's fashion," (237). Neither would she do anything in a Somali man's fashion because the Somali man has let her down. Hana's claim to the idiosyncratic manner of doing things is an unconscious proclamation of the *Western skewed* hybrid identity at which she temporarily stands. The denunciation of betrayal, trouble making and suffering by the Somali man is a feminist notion she has imbibed from the dominant white society. Hana now enjoys the company of white friends, for instance, she goes for a retreat with Helen at *The Hunters,* a ranch and palatial home owned by *carriers*. Rune's clarion call for patience to permit Hana's gradual assimilation does not go down well with Helen who resolves to compel Hana to choose between Western culture and death. She plays the *Jesus Film* and Hana's ethnic identity is ignited. She feels uncomfortable and says, "I really don't need the film to love Jesus. Anyway, I can't see what Jesus got to do with that actor in the film [...] I told you I don't like that film," (264). Helen who has got used to Hana's Western attributes gets shocked and resorts to the use of force. Hana does not budge; she has reverted to the *more ethnic* hybrid identity that rejects Christian influence. Helen plays a documentary that "starts of with news clippings of stolen food convoys by some crazy clansmen somewhere in Somalia" and shouts, "Shame! Shame! Thieves!" (270); it is a racist portrayal of Somalis as lazy thieves. Hana is incensed by the documentary and tells Helen to think about the "Bosnian woman raped and tortured by Christian Serbs to the extent of losing her sense of hearing" (271), yet not a single documentary has been produced to tell the world the story.

Hana is no longer the assimilated passive listener to Helen's stories. Hana goes back to Mulki, a symbolic return to the *ethnic identity* that she has sometimes criticized. The identity shift causes her inner turmoil and sustains psychological problems. When she visits the doctor, his report reveals "a very disturbed young woman behind the pleasant mask" (342), and though we expect her to blame Helen, she skips to her side saying: "My people let me down. And it is them that I should blame, not Helen. By the time I came to the gates of this nation, I was a reject and Helen found a reject. I can't blame her for wanting to take over a reject. So what is the big deal?" (342). Hana is at the ambivalent site where identity as aforementioned depends on the circumstances.

Little Hirsi is another immigrant character the in-between space but unlike Hana, he mostly stands at the *Western skewed* hybrid identity. His name Little Hirsi signifies the two cultural worlds to which he belongs: Western and Somali. He converts to Christianity and supports the *carriers* in their endeavor to assimilate Muslim immigrants "to exact copies of themselves". With excitement, Helen says that Hirsi is "no doubt one of the *carriers*" (147), she knows of what help he has been in her business to turn Muslim youth away from their religion. The claim that Hirsi is a reformed robber, drug addict and a murderer is a concrete fruit of their efforts. He has acquired the English language to bolster his middle ground by interpreting for *carriers* during their evangelistic missions in Mogadishu. Consequently, he moves around the *unreached* world with the *carriers* to facilitate their systemic mode of assimilating immigrants. His appearance validates their credibility to Somali cases being pursued. For Hirsi, his relationship with the *carriers* is invaluable such that although he cannot read, he just receives Helen's pamphlets to please her. In return, they give him and his siblings the much needed material support. He tells Hana that the quicker the immigrant can pick the foreign captive's tongue, "the quicker you can cash your ransom money" (193). His tone is sarcastic, which hints at his attitude towards his Christian faith. The assimilation is just a sham; Hirsi, like Hana and Anisa, is at the ambivalent site. Whenever he meets Hana, he reverts to the *more ethnic* hybrid identity, sometimes mocking Helen and other *carriers*. His identity, like other similar immigrants depends on the social context. No wonder he tells Hana, "game of survival, girl" (193), as a hint to his duplicity. In actual sense of the word, Hirsi's conversion and long testimony of having been a sinner are a ruse to appease the dominant group for material benefits; otherwise he has never reformed. He tells Hana that her "medicine woman" (Helen), has not got the "right remedy" for his sins because there "is a place in his heart" that Helen has never touched" (199), and Hana sympathises with Helen. With Hana, Hirsi is a Somali but with Helen and Jason, he is a "saved Christian" who is quite instrumental in the evangelical vision of the *carriers,* and that is the essence of the *in-between hybrid* identity. As a consequence of this fluctuation on the identity continuum, Little Hirsi has sustained a psychological condition that causes insomnia. He tells Abdirahman that he is "night owl" (346) because "sleep evades" him, so he has to wander in town at night.

Hana's and Anisa's and Hirsi's identity constructions at the in-between space reiterate Ahmed et al views that the process of identity construction overseas "changes according to the immigrants history, position, language and the opposition in their life" (1-2), the immigrant instantly constructs identity depending on the current situation, the choice of words being used by the host and the problems being faced at the moment. As Bhabha asserts, this identity is "unstable element of linkage" (227), it is neither here nor there, not this or that or both, which comes with devastating psychological effects on the immigrant.

3.23 Ethnic Skewed Hybrid Identity

Sulyman interviews a Kurdish immigrant, Lailan about who she is and she replies:

> Sometimes I identify myself as in- between and sometimes more Kurd, but I have never felt a hundred percent as Swede. I identify myself more Kurd and in-between and this depends on the conditions and position that influence and formulate the sense. (20-29)

Sulyman observes that Lailan is "more attached to her Kurdish ethnicity" but factors like "communication, friends, work" (29), that require that she contacts different people compel her to imbibe Swedish culture to manage. Mulki in Abdi's *Offspring of Paradise* falls under this category of *more ethnic* or *ethnic skewed* hybrid identities. She is among the first refugees to arrive at the refugee camp in the Western city and given her higher education background, she enrolls in a language school and lands a job as an interpreter for Somali refugees at the camp. Her love for Somali people is evident in the manner in which she handles Somali refugees, including those from rival clans like Hana and her grandmother. She accepts to be made a servant to Hana and the grandmother when they arrive in the refugee camp, and the loving way in which she looks after them prompts grandmother to make her Hana's guardian. Hana's grandmother assesses Mulki's ethnic identity and her tact to survive in the foreign environment and resolves that she can pass these virtues to the young Hana. Indeed after her death, Mulki stands out as responsible guardian; for instance, she firmly warns Hana against keeping Helen's company. She says:

> She visited you at school? [...] what do you know about this woman, Hana? You are meeting her after school every day. And now she is even coming to school. What's next? This woman is well out of your league. Her record speaks for itself. And that's more than I can say for some ninnies I know who can't even defend their rights... like you, for instance. (102)

Mulki has interacted with the white community at the work place and got background information about Helen; she knows her evil acts of homicide and other misdemeanors that cause Usman's expulsion from school. Worse still, she is aware of the secret cult she works for to convert young Muslims like Hana to Christianity, and given that she loves her ethnic Somali identity, she wants Hana to pattern her life after hers. While at her house, she cooks Somali dishes such as "*anjero, sambossa,* pasta" and listens to songs by Somali singers like Saado Ali,

Khadra Dahir, Hassan Adan Samatar, Umar Duleh, llma Mooge and others that once enthralled the streets of Hamar and Hargeisa," (108-109), and she is filled with nostalgia.

Nonetheless, she interacts with the white people at the work place, and her proficiency in the English language coupled with kindness endears her to her white superiors. She refers to the senior administrator, Rune by the nickname, "Rune *hebel*" (155), to signify the closeness between them. With the community, Mulki is quite friendly with them: she baby sits the neighbours' children during her leisure time and learns how to make "Chilean version of lasagna" (108), from a Chilean neighbor. Mulki also joins a tea party of white women for group counseling. They claim that their doors are "opened to care starved women from third world countries" (117), to offer group therapy but when she joins them, their speeches are quite offensive. They describe immigrant women as bitter and miserable and in one of the meetings they describe female circumcision as "primitive rite" (120), an assertion that Mulki strongly disagrees with. However, being a hybrid, Mulki does not argue, though other women do. She listens and then stops attending the group therapy sessions without any emotional reaction. Unlike the *in-between* hybrids, the *ethnic skewed hybrids* are more stable because they abide by Jaspal and Cinnirella's principle "that identification with the ethnic group has positive implication" (510), since identity is constructed by way of difference.

3.3 Hybrid Identities and the Dominant Group

This section analyses relationship between characters with hybrid identities and with the dominant majority who have different cultural identity. It seeks to analyze the quality of relationships hybrid characters hold with the dominant group in a cosmopolitan environment.

In Abdi's *A Mighty Collision of Two Worlds,* Rako Island comprises of a non-Muslim majority and Muslim minority with the former dominating the past hundreds of years. Sa'id, a radical Muslim at Rako Island, complains that "Christian missionaries have enjoyed total monopoly for the past hundred years" (266) and that is the reason he starts a Muslim organisation to counter their influence. However, Anisa's uncle, Omar, has lived under these conditions throughout his life without lamentations and agitation. As Sister Anne, Anisa's teacher at St. Josephs, reveals, the non Muslim majority have "conspired to keep the Muslim minority at the bottom of the social stratum" (16). Nonetheless, Uncle Omar maintains cordial relations with the Christians and secular majority at the island, neither a quarrel nor a row is recorded between Omar and his non-Muslim neighbours in the story. He takes his niece Anisa to a Catholic mission school where she earns a scholarship to the United States of America as an exchange student. Uncle Omar allows Anisa to go to the West fully aware that the challenges she will face as an immigrant there are similar to those she will confront at Rako Island. He also understands that interacting with Americans will enable Anisa to learn a lot; he therefore remarks that "going to the United States will be an enriching experience" (30). It is his tolerance towards non-Muslims at Rako Island that gives him the nerve to welcome his non-Muslim son-in-law, Mike Paterson. Whereas Anisa's mother describes Mike as a non believing man devoid of godliness and truth, Omar sees him as a truthful and frank man devoid of hypocrisy.

When Anisa enters the middle ground while in the United States of America, there are generally warm relations between her and the white majority. Even Florence her classmate gets used to her prayers, the narrator observes, "Floor had come to accept what she termed her friend's bizarre habits" (49).When she attends discos with Americans, they appreciate her so much that the white American, Mike falls in love with her. At the Latin Food Joint, Charles the Mexican waiter gives her a large glass of fruit punch saying, "especially for miss," (110), as he places it on the table. The fruit punch is a symbol of the strong bond of friendship between Anisa, the Somali-Muslim immigrant and the West. Throughout her courtship period, marriage and honeymoon, Anisa employs cultural hybridity; consequently, there is no disharmony in the marriage, neither do Mike's relatives point a finger at the couple. Apparently, diversity does not create tension between the binary factions, difference does. Mike's mother, his sister, Charlotte and his father seem to have tacitly understood that Mike has married an African American. But as soon as Anisa reverts to cultural fixity or rather ethnic identity, tension arises and mounts. We shall explore this tension in the next chapter when we focus our attention on ethnic identities or cultural fixity.

Mike converts to Islam and becomes a Muslim minority among the dominant non-Muslim white community in the United States of America. His relationship with the white relatives is strained but it does not degenerate to animosity. When his father wants to know why Muslims hate dogs, he explains without taking offence. Mike says that Islam considers a dog's saliva impure and if a Muslim "gets in contact with it, they have to wash seven times" (179). Although the mother gets irritated, Mike explains in a manner that leaves them without offence. Mike takes his mixed race children to his parents and their remarks about Western culture amuse them. Mike's father says of little Mohamed, "[t]he poor fellow said Allah."

"[w]here is Allah," I said.

["g]randpa, watch out what you say about Allah, beware you are grandpa! God what kind of grandpa is this!" (406), the grandparents roar with laughter, and this is a sign of the amity between Mike and his white parents brought about by the hybrid children. His sister, Charlotte, reserves her time to babysit the children. Mike does not defend Anisa when his parents make negative remarks about her (395); it is clear that he detests her rigidness when dealing with the West. Nevertheless, he engages in healthy discussions when the parents question Islam as a result of cultural diversity, for instance, when his mother observes that the Quran is a plagiarized version of the Bible, Mike wishes to know "which version of the Bible has been plagiarized because Christians have many versions of it" (397). In all this, the arguments are carried out peaceably with the two groups learning from each other, there is no violence between Mike and his parents. Mohamed and Nasra therefore have cordial relations with both Muslims at Rako Island and the white community in the United States. When their father takes them to the United States of America, they note differences between the West and the East and bring light moments for the families and while at Rako Island, they miss their white father. When they go to the United States, they miss their mother, Anisa so much that it compels Mike to return to Rako Island, reuniting him with his wife.

The community speaker at Rako Island consults the personal secretary to accost the president when Sa'id and Usman are arrested on trumped charges. The personal secretary is a Muslim but has forged strong bonds of friendship with non-Muslims in Rako Island. By virtue of being appointed personal secretary is a sign of trust, in a nation where non-Muslims have schemed to subjugate Muslims; he has risen to the position of a confidante of the non-Muslim leader and at this point in time, an "indispensable representative of his community" (283-284). Although the Muslim pedants like Sa'id see him as a traitor, he turns out to be the only one that can assist to negotiate their release after being detained. He discusses the matter with the president and they are released. The secretary who has lived at the middle ground has a rapport with non Muslims and is able to fight more effectively for his community than those that embrace cultural fixity like Sa'id and Usman.

In *Offspring of Paradise,* characters with hybrid identities maintain friendly relationships with the dominant group. Although he hails from the marginalized clan, Mulki's father loves the ruling clan and marries among them. When his clansmen start persecuting the ruling clan during the ensuing political strife, he keeps his distance. He is so much disappointed by his sons who join the militia group to persecute their mother's relatives. Abdullah, one of his sons, refuses to protect Zahra, their mother's relative, in spite of his effort to tell him "it is not Zahra's fault that she was who she was" (34). He therefore criticizes his son's acts of polarity and assaults him. Mulki's father is only hostile towards his son in the course displaying his great love for the clan considered by many of his relatives as *fagash* or loyalists. His daughter, Mulki, takes after him by the manner in which she maintains friendly relationships with the dominant group both in Somalia and overseas. She loves the ruling clan in Somalia and that explains why she befriends Zahra while studying at the university. The narrator says that when the clan warfare began, "both Mulki and Zahra were pursuing undergraduate courses in the national university at Hamar" (16), and so when Zahra learns of her uncle's assassination, she runs to Mulki for refuge. Her family (like Hana's) is "an offshoot of the president's ethnic group and is branded *fagash*- loyalists" (16) who deserve death. Although militia men (Mulki's clansmen) are in their home with Mulki's brothers, Mulki takes the risk of hosting Zahra, in her bedroom. She shuts the door of her bedroom and signaling Zahra against speaking, "lets her in through the window" (18). Her love for the dominant clan drives her to plead with Abdullah, her brother, to protect Zahra; she had earlier on promised Zahra's mother that she would look after Zahra. Her desire to care for Zahra is not fulfilled following her disappearance on the way out of Magadishu and she transfers this desire to Hana in overseas. Mulki and her mother are among the first refugees in *the wall*. She enrolls in a language school and gets a job as an interpreter at the refugee camp. It is while interpreting for Rune, *the wall* administrator, when she walks into the eight-year old Hana and her grandmother, *Ayeyo*.

The relationship between Mulki and Hana, and the white community is undoubtedly cordial. In spite of Hana's emotional tantrums, more often accusing Mulki of abandoning Zahra, Mulki holds her head and guides her to grow as a good Muslim. She understands that having lost a close relation, Hana has a right to strong feelings. Whatever Hana says, Mulki knows that she is the guardian hence duty bound to guide her into responsible adulthood. She does not see her as a greedy *fagash* as her brother Abdullah would have seen but as a daughter to be taught discipline and other aspects of responsible adulthood. There is warm if not affable relationship between Mulki and the white community, her open mind enabling her to join the tea party of white ladies in the neighbourhood. It is here that she learns that they harbor prejudice towards black people. They view black female attendants as "lonely sisters" (117) who go there to share their painful experiences for therapeutic reasons. Mulki does not even argue when a visiting doctor at the meeting denounces female circumcision as a "primitive rite". She stops attending the tea party meetings but later learns that tea party women themselves got tired of it" (120).

Using this knowledge, she guides Hana about the need to be cautious in their relationship with white people like Helen Banister. Mulki wants Hana to first develop an ethnic identity before acquiring attributes of Western culture to evade psychological consequences of in-between identity. That is the reason she warns her against rushing into friendship with the white *carrier* Helen. She says, "[a]bout this woman, who is she? [...] How would she know of your mother?"(104). Hana rebels and arranges many dates with Helen only to regret later. It is Mulki's exemplary rapport with the white community that prompts the administration at the *wall* to entrust her with Hana and her grandmother. The "youthful immigrants pouring into the Western city" are prospective converts to Christianity and their names are entered into "special files such as A files, B files, I files, mortal files and many others" (40). Hana is therefore a target and it would be daft to place her under custody of a fixed character; Rune selects the hybrid, Mulki; a hybrid immigrant who can hand down the alien attributes she has learnt from whites to Hana. She is already fluent in the English language and if all other attributes fail she can at least pass this on.

Little Hirsi is a youthful immigrant most denigrated by Muslim characters in *Offspring of Paradise*. He too looks down upon himself, for instance, he tells Hana that he is "a born loser" (344). On the contrary, Hirsi is a go-getter given his determination to acquire material benefits for his family and himself by the way he relates with the white community. He is the beloved of the *carriers* always by Jason's side as a Somali interpreter on his journeys in Mogadishu besides being used by the *carriers* as a religious pawn to woo young Muslims to Christianity. In return, they give him love and material support; Helen is elated by this that she asserts, "[h]e is one of us free and frank" (147). In a dramatic irony, we are meant to understand that Hirsi's *Western skewed hybrid* identity is a ruse to coexist in a cosmopolitan society. He tells Hana that "a foreign tongue is a weapon without which an African immigrant cannot acquire wealth" (193). He astounds the reader when he reveals that he has never converted to Christianity when he declares that there are parts of him that Helen "has never touched" (199) which is a reference to his spiritual life that is still indebted to Islam. Hana also employs cultural hybridity and hence maintains a cordial relationship with the dominant group. At the in-between space, not a grain of violence is manifested in her dealings with the *carriers*. They have a benevolent friendship with Helen until Helen unveils her counterfeit hybridity. Hana has never abandoned her Islamic faith, even as she goes to church, shakes Rune's hand, abandons the *hijab* (all of which run counter to Islamic tradition), she still prays five times a day. As observed in the previous chapter, she is at the ambivalent site to facilitate her existence in the cosmopolitan society. She defends Helen against Usman's criticism and reminds him the failures of the Somali brother who "dumps his sister in the cold" and starts trailing her around (230). When Helen turns against her, she pretends to have surrendered to bolster the friendship and then befriends Mrs. Grant, a white servant at *the Hunters*. As Helen is still in her self-deluding excitement, Mrs. Grant helps her to flee thereby saving her life.

Like Mike in *A Mighty Collision of Two Worlds*, Rune in *Offspring of Paradise* defies the essentialist white majorities who have formed a cult to turn African immigrants "into their carbon copies" (348), and forges genuine friendships with Muslim minorities. After he enters the middle ground, the white community becomes uneasy with him; nonetheless, his relationship with them does no degenerate into animosity. Rune reads a lot about Islam and Christianity and is therefore aware that Christians should give without expecting anything in return. He disapproves the *carriers'* ploy to do good to Muslim immigrants in order to compel them into submission to Christianity. He is also aware that since they are poorly read, they lack essential information about Islam. Rune wants to get Helen out of his plan to find Hana's mother to register his disapproval. He tells Mulki: "I want you to tell Hana to sit tight and let me handle this and have the pleasure of putting the woman away for good. But not until I have Hana's mother safely here. You see I am sending a friend over to Hamar" (322). During the *carriers'* meeting; Rune steals Jason's show by opposing their counterfeit hybridity. He warns against haste and advocates "good works, charity, clarity of purpose and prayer as virtues that ambassadors of Christianity ought to have" (179). Patience, he adds is key to the business of soul winning, but haste not only adulterates, it but is also in contravention to teachings of the Christian religion. Although some like Helen detest his strategy, most *carriers* revere him. Jason, Helen's lover regards him and "blesses him" when he talks to Hana (155). He knows that his likable character would influence Hana to convert. Rune's hybridity turns him into a prized asset to the *carriers*. He is neither at logger heads with *carriers* nor immigrants thereby the best instrument of reaching out to Muslim immigrants. He asserts that he has won some immigrants to Christianity, "[s]ometimes we win on the spot, sometimes we win later," (206). Patience should be the mantra, he insists. Infuriated by Rune's opposition, Helen arranges Rune's abduction and he goes missing for some days. The police are dispatched to interrogate Hana and this is the worst Rune comes to in his relationship with the majority.

To sum up therefore, hybrid characters have cordial relationships with the dominant group despite the risks involved. There is no tension, anxiety and physical confrontation observed when the minority opt for hybridity as a strategy of resistance. Characters of diverse hybrid identities like Mike, Anisa, Hana and Rune relate affably with the dominant group as opposed to *counterfeit* hybrids such as Helen who mechanically apply hybridity to manipulate others and therefore flop. Abdi denigrates this self imposed kind of hybrid identity, the type embraced by Helen and suggests that it is fixity concealed behind the veil of hybridity.

3.4 Conclusion

In the light of foregoing analysis hybridity plays a very significant role in the construction of identity of migrant characters because we observe in the first section characters shifting from their ethnic identities into the in-between space due to the impact of Western culture. Anisa, in *A Mighty Collision of Two Worlds* arrives in Fairwood School in the United States deeply rooted in Somali and Islamic traditions but with time, she embraces American traditions so much that she marries an American atheist. Hana and Little Hirsi in *Offspring of Paradise* take a similar pattern. In the second section, the chapter dwelt on the analysis of hybrid identities in Abdi's fiction: *Shared sense* hybrid identities, identities that exhibit two cultures in an equal measure; *in-between hybrid* identities, identities characterized by extreme ambivalence; *Western skewed* hybrid identities, identities in which character lean towards Western culture and *ethnic skewed* hybrid identities, identities characterized by leaning towards Somali culture. In this section, it was noted that apart from the in-between hybrid identity, the other forms of hybridity do not have negative psychological effects on the migrant characters. The chapter came to a close with the analysis of the relationship between hybrid characters and the dominant communities. It was interesting to note that all hybrid characters had a cordial relationship with the dominant community at that instant when they were hybrids. Some characters, such as Anisa experience both cordial and strained relationships because of ambivalence typical of the in-between hybrid identity, which makes her vulnerable to hybridity and fixity that attract the two contradictory reactions from the dominant group.

CHAPTER FOUR

Hybridity and Fixity as Modes of Resistance

Introduction

Immigrants who arrive in foreign countries choose various ethnic identities to coexist with the dominant group and resist domination by the host majority. Social scientists distinguish ethnic identity from ethnicity; they postulate that the former can change according to the immigrant's environment and the choices he makes but the latter is quite fixed, given its inherent determinants. Citing Max Weber, Wittich Claus and Roth Guenther who defines ethnic groups as "those human beings that entertain a subjective belief in their common decent because of similarities of physical type or of customs or both or because of memories of colonization and migration" (389), which is therefore a permanent characteristic of the host country. Nevertheless, ethnic identity is flexible; Epstein Gil and Odelia Hezler define it "as a measurement of the feeling of belonging to a particular ethnic group" (2), and single out *ethnosizer* as the appropriate method of measuring ethnic identity. The scholars observe that *ethnosizer* employs language, culture, social interaction, history of migration and ethnic self identification to classify immigrants into four major states: assimilation, integration, separation and marginalization. Amelie and Klaus define the four states: assimilation is "strong identification with the receiving country's culture and weak identification with the country of origin", integration is "a strong bond with the country of origin with simultaneous strong connection with receiving country" (5), while separation is " identification with original culture, even years after emigration" (5), and finally Marginalisation is having "no sense of belonging neither to receiving country's culture nor to that of original country" (5). Assimilation, integration, separation and marginalization are four ethnic identities that immigrants adapt when they reach overseas and each determines the quality of relationship they have with the dominant majority. In the present study, characters that integrate and assimilate choose cultural hybridity while those that separate themselves from the majority choose cultural fixity as a mode of resistance. Abdi's characters do not choose marginalization as a mode of resistance overseas.

The principal characters in this chapter are Hana, Abdirahman, Mulki and Helen in *Offspring of Paradise* and Anisa, Yusuf, Usman, Sa'id, Nasra and Khadija in *A Mighty Collision of Two Worlds*. Hana is the immigrant who arrives in a Western city at the tender age of eight in *Offspring of Paradise* and she becomes prey to the Christian evangelists that are bent on assimilating young immigrants. Helen is the Christian evangelist tasked with the responsibility of converting Hana; she works for a Christian organization called *carriers*. Abdirahman is a Muslim cleric that teaches Somali children to memorize the Holy Quran and arranges classes to equip Muslims with knowledge to counter Western influence at the refugee camp and Mulki is Hana's guardian at the refugee camp. When the Somalia civil war breaks out, Mulki is a university student in a national university in Somalia, and so she integrates rapidly in the foreign country. Anisa is the heroine in *A Mighty Collision of Two Worlds* and the youthful immigrant that arrives in the United States from Rako Island in her puberty on a school exchange program. Yusuf is the Muslim cleric who guides Anisa when she suffers psychologically after marrying Mike, the white American atheist. Yusuf leads Mike in conversion to Islam and gives him religious books to ground him in the Islamic faith. Sa'id is a Muslim faithful with radical views at Rako Island; he forms a Muslim association to counter domination of secular and Christian majority at the Island. Usman is Sa'id's friend; they are arrested together for exhibiting extremist views that destabilize the peace of the island. Nasra is Anisa's and Mike's first born child, a mixed race child with attachment to Western and Eastern cultures. This chapter compares and contrasts cultural fixity and cultural hybridity as strategies of resistance applied by immigrant characters in Abdi's fiction. The chapter will analyze the merits and demerits of each strategy and settle on the better of the two. It will start by tracing the relapse of some immigrant characters to fixity and how it affects their relationships with the dominant white majority. Characters with fixed identities (those that choose separation) and their relationship with the dominant group will be analysed. The chapter will end by examining the merits and demerits of each strategy and then single out the better of the two.

4.1 Relapse to Cultural Fixity and the Shift in Relationships

Racial minority groups such as black children grow up internalizing the white dominant attitudes and behaviors assimilating to white dominant culture in order to pass. The process of naturalization and essentialisation of self identity in relation to the other and the fictive determination of sameness and difference- who gets to be included and who gets to be excluded cause profound pain and ambivalence in the oppressed. The subject who constantly oscillates between cultures takes on a double consciousness, and it heavily influences one's communicative practices. (Chiang, 31)

In the above extract, Yun Chih Chiang explores the effect of Western culture on immigrant children. Abdi's characters such as Anisa and Hana arrive in the West at tender ages and imbibe white dominant culture in order to acquire education and fit in the foreign community. The ensuing process of constructing hybrid identity, at the in-between space causes the "profound pain," the psychological trauma, which results from constant shift from one end of the identity continuum to the other. Chiang's "double consciousness" refers to "the in-between" hybrid identity (expounded in the previous section), which is characterized by instability. This section concerns itself with those characters that adopt the *in-between* hybrid identity and how their relationships with the dominant group change with it. The undulation between *ethnic skewed* identity and *Western skewed* identity comes with shift in relationships.

In *Offspring of Paradise,* Hana opens her arms to embrace the white people soon after her grandmother's demise, taking the white woman, Helen for a bosom friend. *Ayeyo,* as grandmother is called, is the embodiment of the past tradition and her death signifies the end of obsession with the past. Hana arranges dates with Helen in different rendezvous at Mulki's utter shock. Helen takes the pains of going to school to pick Hana up to take her out in expensive hotels. Having relegated her people and traditions, Helen appreciates and dotes on Hana. The two friends have a cordial or rather doting relationship and exchange many things. Mulki realizes that Hana cannot prepare "authentic Somali tea" (109), using a Somali recipe, worse still, they rarely have time together to allow Hana to learn from the older. Hana is getting assimilated by the foreign culture; Helen is elated. She is glad as long as the immigrant is ceding ground to embrace Christian principles at the expense of Islam. She studies and learns about the hostility among Somali clans and seizes the moment to sow discord between Mulki and Hana. She says, "[h]ow could you trust these people

(Mulki's clan)? After all they did to you? They killed your folks" [...] (142). Helen describes Mulki as a war lord's cousin that will not be of any help to her. She therefore offers to get a good house for Hana to keep off from Mulki. Amelie Constant et al observe that "assimilated and integrated immigrants are more likely to own a house than those who are separated or marginalized" (3-30).

It follows that Hana's friendship owes to her high degrees of assimilation as a result of cultural hybridity. Walters David et al note that "as social socio-cultural assimilation occurs and values and attitudes of newcomers converge with those of the native population, barriers to full economic participation will break down" (2). Helen's offer of house is a pointer to her readiness to give Hana anything of worth she can afford but for her minor status. Helen's sudden appeal to ethnicity or rather cultural fixity magnifies difference thereby compelling Hana to shift her ground. Richard Jenkins observes that ethnicity is "about cultural differentiation" (165), and that is why one would like to interpret how Hana projects her ethnicity to combat Helen's appeal to fixity as a move towards such "differentiation". She rejects the offer of accommodation and chooses to live with Mulki. Hana asserts that in spite of rivalry among Somalis, they are one family. Citing *Ayeyo's* words, she tells Helen:

> Some of us may seem to you like cutthroats, but at the end of the day, we're family, and especially here in the wall. You could say that we've got here nothing more than sibling rivalry gone awry if you will. This is definitely what you would call a war...nobody wins here. (143)

After this speech, Helen is mesmerized by her wisdom but is displeased because Hana seems grounded in ethnicity courtesy of her grandmother that will enable her to evade Helen's trap. Helen knows quite well that her decision to quote Ayeyo's words symbolizes the relapse to ethnicity, which is a marker of cultural fixity. Her grandmother had compared Somalia violence to sibling rivalry in the family, "a war none can win" (143). Hana declares that she does not need Helen's assistance to resist Mulki, an assertion that irritates Helen. As they turn to their ethnicity, they erect binary factions; tension mounts and their friendship is strained. Rune intervenes to advise Helen against the cultural essentialism, behind Helen's rashness and impatience. He observes that Hana has "lost everything except her religion" (322), and she needs more time to let it go. Rune implies that Hana is not assimilated but integrated, where she appreciates both identities. Helen rejects Rune's advice saying that Abdirahman is after Hana and the longer she waits the higher the chances of losing her. Henceforth, Helen discards her "counterfeit hybridity" and embraces her real self, which is cultural essentialism. She adores her Western culture so much and has just befriended Hana to convert her. She gives Hana her mother's picture saying "if you refuse to co-operate, it will be bye bye" (209). She means that Hana will only to benefit from her if she assimilates. Helen's hatred for Rune escalates so much that she plots his abduction. It is not astounding to the reader when Rune is reported "missing" (215). The police are dispatched to interrogate Hana after which Helen kidnaps her too. She induces her into sleep and drives to a distant ranch, *the Hunters*. At the palatial home, Helen, obsessed with cultural essentialism, is prepared to impose her culture on Hana. She reduces everything to 'us' and 'them', a difference that is typical of cultural essentialism. Helen and her fellow *carriers* see themselves as a nation, defined by Lotle Jensen as "a subjective community established by shared culture and historical memories, not only involving sense of belonging but also being distinct from others" (7).

They view themselves as distinct from Somali refugees, in physique and culture, and Helen's appeal to these primordial differences widens the gap between her and Hana. Helen reckons that because Hana has refused to become a Christian, she does not care about her. Their conversation at the *Hunters* is followed by succession of Christian films, Helen interrupting the watching with awesome exclamations about the suffering of Jesus. Hana does not find the suffering of Jesus pertinent to her religious beliefs given her Islamic beliefs that deny the crucifixion and resurrection of Issa (Jesus); the difference gradually widens. Responding to fixity by fixity, Hana declares that she does not want to be forced to watch films she "is not interested in" (266). Some of the documentaries portray African immigrants as thieves, prompting Helen to shout, "[s]hame, shame!" (270). Gradually, Hana relapses to cultural essentialism and adopts separation as strategy of resistance apparently because of Helen's appeal to it. Amelie and Klaus observe that immigrants choose separation when host communities segregate them from mainstream society. The scholars write, "[t]he openness of people in the new country, their embracing of new culture and their respect towards the newcomers can play a major role in how immigrants react and how close they remain with the country of origin" (5). Helen's initial respect for Hana with her friends, embracing her culture by attending Abdirahman's classes yielded a positive reaction from Hana. Helen employs a cultural hybridity however counterfeit and it draws Hana closer to Christianity. But when she appeals to fixity, Hana retreats to her original culture. Infuriated, Helen declares furiously that "it is payback time" (267) and Hana has to choose between conversion and death. She utters a tantrum, referring to Abdirahman as "a spade bearded man" and Mulki as "the silly woman who plays mother to Hana" (268). As she jeers at callous African characters, Hana reminds her that Christian Serbs had raped and tortured a Bosnian woman until she had lost "a sense of hearing" (271), but she wonders why no documentary had been produced to show the world. Compelled to embrace her ethnicity, Hana utters what appears to be a defense of her culture; she asserts that there is international conspiracy to besmirch the reputation of African immigrants.

The East and West get locked in a binary opposition and tension rises. The tension between the former bosom friends breaks into open confrontation; Helen determined not to lose the 'project'. She tells Hana that the white people "feed the immigrants, clothe them and therefore own their lives" (270). She even reveals that Hana has been on the *carrier's* list, a project she has pursued so long. It is with profound shock that Hana realizes that she has just been a lifeless project in Helen's life. In the same vein, she retorts that she is not interested in being on anyone's list. Helen flounces away incensed and their relationship sours further. Hana is downcast because for a long time she has deluded herself in a relationship in which she is no better than a project. Her dream of integration and eventual assimilation into the privileged white society is rendered futile. She concludes that an immigrant will never be accepted by the host community. She compares the immigrant to "an unbranded cow among a branded herd" (276), appeals to cultural fixity have beyond reasonable doubt ruined their relationship.

In *A Mighty Collision of Two Worlds,* Anisa marries Mike while at the hybrid space where she has chosen integration to coexist in the cosmopolitan society. After three months of marriage, she starts complaining that Mike should convert as he had promised. Mike gives way and converts to Islam, picking the name "Ali Ahmed Paterson" (162), a symbol of hybridity. In one of her visits to Yusuf, a Muslim cleric, a scripture from the Holy Quran is shared. The verse becomes a turning point in Anisa's life: "And do not marry idolaters until they believe…and do not give believing women in marriage to idolaters," (142). Yusuf holds that Anisa's marriage cannot work and should be dissolved. The words heighten Anisa's doubts both in herself as a Muslim and her marriage to the atheist.

Overwhelmed by the guilt of deliberately abandoning her identity, she embarks on the process of reconstructing it by reverting to extremities. Mike has to brush his teeth before breakfast. He has to use water at the loos, he has to use the left hand to take food and "there is no breakfast in bed" (164). Anisa refuses any compromises by inflexibly laying down the law as prescribed in the Holy Quran. She extends the Eastern traditions to Mike's extended family by looking down on their festivities; for instance, she isolates herself from "Christmas and Easter" celebrations. She frowns at "Halloween witchery", which she refers to as "archaic, pagan tradition" (168). One day, Mike's mother brings Nasra, a dog for a present, the puppy licks Nasra's feet and Anisa hysterically rejects the gift. Mike's mother is so infuriated in spite of Mike's intervention to abate the situation. Mike tells his mother to respect Anisa's way of life but the white relatives angrily denounce her given her stubborn refusal to compromise. They no longer appreciate Anisa because she reverts to separation and lauds her ethnic traditions, which are different from those of the host community. By appealing to cultural essentialism, she exposes herself to discrimination in her marriage.

Dr M.K. Gautam observes that although ethnicity restores immigrants "suspended identity, its reliance on ancestral ties, kinship relations, common language and religious beliefs is a baggage that exposes immigrants to the host community and government" (7). Anisa has restored her ethnic identity but her glaring differences from mode of dress, manner of prayer and other Islamic mannerisms make her an easy target to the white community. Mike's mother attacks, declaring that "the black alien has taken over their life, even calling Mike some barbaric names" (169). Charlotte, Mike's sister, remarks that Anisa is "out of her league, a misfit who cannot survive in the American society" (170). Apparently it is the whites to compromise for she will not even celebrate the baby's birthday because it is irreligious. Mike's mother says:

> Everything's forbidden, everything', she said pacing up and down her cushy living room." We can't even have a decent family get together without consultations as to what to put on the dinner table! The whole thing stinks. You may keep that woman but as far as we're concerned it's over... Force it on her? I have every right to celebrate my grand child's birthday, and with whatever takes my fancy! She has no right to take that away from me!' (177)

Consequently, Charlotte cuts loose from Mike's family and his mother declares that Anisa is some sort of anti-Christ that casts aspersions at Jesus. She complains that Anisa "does not believe in the Lord Jesus" (174). She laments that they can no longer have family parties because for Anisa, everything is forbidden. She declares that her relationship with Mike is over, to cap it all, she proclaims herself a white person whose badge is Christianity and would not take orders from a black alien daughter-in-law.

Like Helen in *Offspring of Paradise,* Anisa turns to separation or cultural essentialism, which introduces Islam to her Western hosts but ruins her friendly relations with the West. The more she appeals to separation, the worse the relationship becomes even with the very Mike she has recently introduced Islam to. Impatiently, she levels false accusations at Mike: "he cannot stand his Muslim name, he accepted the faith just to marry her, he only prays while with Yusuf, he never has a good word about Muslims, he makes fun of Arabs and he hates Christians" (194). Just as Rune advises Helen, Khadija prevails upon Anisa to be patient with Mike but she refuses. Anisa regrets having integrated, she condemns herself: "[s]ince the day I came to this country I'd been leading a double life except a few times I'd been at home" (197). She remembers Yusuf's instruction and sees herself as a sinner who messed around with her faith. Guilt takes a heavy toll on her life. In attempt to restore her religious identity, she appeals to cultural essentialism, and the ensuing pain drives her to insanity. She cautions Mike against taking "the children to his pagan parents" (213). In six weeks, she skids into a total mental breakdown. She is admitted but the psychiatrist is irritated by her tirades at the Christian beliefs. Anisa is obsessed with difference and degrading discrimination in the cosmopolitan society. She tells the doctor that "Jesus started as a prophet, promoted to a son of God and elevated to God in heaven" (220). The doctor exhorts her to moderate her obsession to pave way for her recovery. Anisa staggers around shouting the *shahada* "to scare away every jinni". After discharge and partial recovery, she puts on a scarf everywhere to symbolize her relapse into cultural fixity. Mike is embarrassed before his friends owing to his wife's queer scarf. She tells

Mike that "she must rid herself all duplicity" (235). She says: "[m]y hair and body belong to me and no one else. I am not public property, not anymore. And if people find it so odious then that is their problem. I want to be me. I've just found myself and am not letting go off me. This is natural me," (236). Mike is surprised at her obsession with ethnicity; she cannot handle a conversation without reference to it. She tells Mike to speak to children in a religious register. He has to mention Allah to them and after each meal they must say "*Alhamdulillah*" (237). A few weeks after discharge, she gives Mike a condition to accept Islam fundamentally or forfeit the marriage.

Anisa's appeal to fixity prompts Mike to opt for extremes; he calls her "a Muslim fanatic". She gives him Bibles but "he throws them at her" (243). Like Helen, her efforts to impose her way of life on others fail and so she abducts the children and flees to Rako Island. This is a symbolic journey to rediscover herself in the East, a symbolic Return to a fixed identity that Hall disputes. For Hall, the Uncle Omar Anisa returns at Rako Island, has changed because he is not the rigid person she might have known. Indeed, even as Anisa condemns the West to her Rakon audiences, uncle Omar does not buy it. Anisa tells tales of Western faithlessness, that the people "worship painkillers and tranquilizers" (276). Her tales are alibi to validate the delusion that there can be no marriage between her and the faithless Mike. Nonetheless, Uncle Omar reminds her that her attempt to impose Islam on Mike is the root cause of the marital problems. He says that Mike is a promising Muslim and remains his son-in-law. He cautions that it would be unfair to terminate the marriage without involving Mike. Furthermore, he has not been given time to nurture his Islamic faith. Uncle Omar discredits Anisa's appeals to fixity: "[n]o one can force Islam. The messenger of Allah could not convince his own dear uncles. Learn from that fact," (310). Anisa's attempt to force Mike is therefore prohibited in Islam and is the author seems to suggest that it is she has borrowed from the West given that the strategy parallels the *carriers'* in *Offspring of Paradise*. Uncle Omar recommends that she writes a letter to Mike. She writes the letter to symbolize her transition from ethnicity back to cultural hybridity. As she reverts to hybridity, there is a shift in relationships from acrimony to affability.

4.2 Fixed Identities and the Dominant Group

Cultural essentialism has far reaching consequences on immigrants and host community. Kon K. Madut investigates the impact of ethnicity on the Canadian cosmopolitan society where social integration is hampered by a segmented essentializing system that has polarised society. He writes:

> When it comes to inner perceptions of ethnicity, categorization and marginalization, we find that Canadian society cleaves along four distinct ethnic groups: (1) Anglophone (2) Francophone (3) First Nations (4) Visible minority communities. This social structure is upheld by misinterpretation of policies of Multicultural Act of 1986 that encourages communities to remain socially, culturally and ethnically distinct. In this scheme, English and French were named as official languages but it does not prevent immigrants from speaking and writing vernaculars hence widening the social interaction gap between minorities and majorities. (27)

The overemphasis on cultural essentialism and separate development deludes African and Asian immigrants (visible immigrants) to embrace their cultures and become easy targets of discrimination by the dominant white majority. It was the same policy that was applied in South Africa during the apartheid regime; separate development of different races was emphasized thereby making Africans vulnerable to discrimination. Madut notes that "the Ethnicity Diversity Survey conducted in 2004 in Canada revealed that thirty six percent of visible minorities have been subjected to discrimination because of their race, language and religion, fifty six percent of whom are discriminated at the work place" (89). Research in migration proves that harmonious coexistence between immigrants and the dominant group is only possible where the immigrants are integrated via cultural hybridity. Tendencies towards cultural essentialism or separation result in hostility among various groups. Gautam writes:

> Integration is observed when a different ethnic group accepts norms of the host society, behaves like them but can retain its ethnic culture, social system, language and religious beliefs [...] but when the group becomes a visible phenomenon, it can face some sort of discrimination from the host culture. It could be due to conflict or competition which can show cracks in the social process of co-operation. (3)

Gautam suggests that cultural hybridity reduces tension between the minorities and the dominant majority but cultural fixity results in conflicts that tear the social fabric of the immigration state. He cites incidents of violence in which "eight Indian immigrants were attacked in Muglen near the city of Leipzig in Germany" (24), and when they organized a peaceful demonstration, German whites were heard shouting, "[f]oreigners, leave Germany." Ethnicity or cultural fixity is squarely to blame for the tense and subsequent violent relationship between the Indian immigrants and the German host communities. Gautama observes that Indian immigrants "still remain inencapsulated in their own community and are not well integrated with their host society" (27), making it absolutely problematic for the host community to relate with them. Citing Kipling's poem, he expresses the host community's desperation:

> The stranger within my gate
> He may be true or kind,
> But he does not talk my talk.
> I cannot feel his mind.
> I see the face, and the eyes and the mouth,
> But not the soul behind.
> The men of my own stock,
> They may do ill or well,
> But they tell me lies I wonted to.
> They are used to the lies I tell,
> And we do not need interpreters,
> When we go to buy or sell. (27)

Kipling's poem reveals what becomes of the immigrants when they adopt cultural fixity or separation. The persona, a white host expresses his inability to interact with the immigrants because of their failure to integrate in the host community. The immigrant does not know the hosts' language (does not talk my talk) and so the two groups can neither share ideas nor trade. He would rather interact with fellow hosts however depraved since they share a tongue (and we do not need interpreters). The language barrier creates a gap in communication between white hosts and immigrants; subsequently the two communities replace dialogue failure with tension and violence. Amelie and Klaus observe that "riots and clashes between immigrants and the police in Britain in the eighties compelled the government to reconsider its nonchalant multicultural stance and enforced the learning of language, culture, history and values if immigrants want to stay in Britain" (11). The British government had to retract the lousy multicultural policy that encouraged cultural fixity (ethnicity) and opted for integration (hybridity) to abate the tension between the dominant white majority and immigrants. In Abdi's novels, there are migrant characters that choose cultural ethnicity over integration in immigration nations, which affects their relationships with the dominant white hosts. This section will concern itself with analysis of these characters and the way they relate with the dominant majority.

The character Abdirahman in *Offspring of Paradise* does not waver in his fidelity of belief in ethnic traditions. He has chosen the path of separation, identifying himself with Somali culture, after living many years in the Western city. At the *Wall*, where Somali refugees live, he is the embodiment of both the Somali and Islamic traditions and many immigrants look up to him for restoration of ethnic identity. He is Hana's Quranic teacher that has left a lasting impact on the student; she tells Helen that "Abdirahman is different, he is a man of God" (187). He is a teacher of the Islamic religion and arranges seminars to impart knowledge among the immigrants. Helen attends some of his classes and is scared by his sterling determination, piety and wealth of knowledge. He encourages Muslim immigrants that the Somali predicament stems from their insistence on violating Allah's commandments. Allah lets them "pass through trials for breaking rules" (187), which restores Hana's faith in her people. He also disapproves Hana's choice of hotel, contending that he does not expect a serious Muslim like Hana to be "found in such a secular place" (230). He therefore implies that a practicing Muslim should visit the mosque; keep Muslim friends and shun secular environments. He disapproves Hana's attempts at integration and exhorts her to choose cultural fixity. Consequently, Abdirahman does not coexist peacefully with the white majority. Helen who represents the Christian majority in town detests Abdirahman and wants Hana to steer clear of him. She says if she were Hana, "she would not take his lessons seriously" (187), because he underscores cultural essentialism or ethnicity, which magnifies the difference between immigrants and the host community. At the church, Helen tells Rune that unless they work harder to convert Hana, Abdirahman, "the bearded fundamentalist would grab her" (207). Hana notes that Helen is always exasperated when Abdirahman is within their precincts. One day she blurts, "[h]e can't fool me that man with a goatee" (188).

Abdirahman's choice of ethnicity eats into his relationships with the dominant majority group and in fact there is no other job the white community can offer him save for preaching at the refugee camp because of the suspicion, tension and hostility between him and the white majority at *the wall*. Amelie and Klaus observe that "with regards to religion, the non religious immigrants earn the most [...] separated immigrants are confined in the ethnic enclaves with low prospects of being incorporated in the host country and being successful" (13). Abdirahman is therefore confined within Somali social circles perpetuating ethnicity and the polarity that come with it. Usman is referred to as the *Fourth party* in the story. He is the Somali young man that trails Hana and Little Hirsi whenever they are in company, when he finds her alone, he warns her against keeping Helen's company. He reveals that he was once Helen's friend but their relationship came to a bitter end. Usman is an example of immigrants who according to Zimmermann and Amelie, are willing to integrate but the host community is neither open nor respectful to the new comers" (5). Usman therefore reverts to his ethnicity and constantly discourages fellow immigrants from assimilating. He tells Hana that Helen "is not sincere and is only using Hana to satisfy a personal obsession" (228) and her life would go waste. When Hana remains adamant, he invites Abdirahman, her Quranic teacher, to talk to her. Usman believes that integration and assimilation in the immigration nation is no good for Hana and ought to choose separation or cultural fixity Abdirahman. As a result of his love for ethnicity, the white community detests him. Helen calls him "an ungrateful fellow that shadows around her" (207). Usman has lost any economic privileges that Helen may have accessed her to, such as finding her job. He is one those immigrants who according to Amelie and Zimmermann separation denies economic participation in the host nation. Helen distastes his determined resolve to filch young Somalis from her claws, hence creating mistrust between Usman and the dominant group.

In *A Mighty Collision of Two Worlds,* Sa'id, Faiza's husband is more concerned with cultural essentialism than integration and assimilation. He believes that Islam should be practiced in all its purity and those Muslims that embrace some aspects of Western culture are charlatans. As young man, he goes abroad and never sets foot in a disco joint; he rejects secular music and frowns at white people's culture. Those Muslims that have embraced aspects of western culture have lost pure Islam and should renew their commitments to the religion. He calls them "Muslim hypocrites" (84) and goes a step farther to join an organization to conduct "Islamization of these Muslims back to the pure faith" (84). Gautam emphasizes the role of associations among minorities in a cosmopolitan community. He writes:

> Individuals with shared ideas and memory come together and form associations to retain their cultural security. When individuals are confronted with derogatory unpleasant remarks and some sort of unforeseen discrimination, the scattered members of the ethnic group gather conduct informal meetings and decide to establish associations. The difference becomes big when the host community uses the terms "we" and "they." (4)

Rako Island is a cosmopolitan society comprised of minority Muslims and dominant secular and Christian majority. The latter have for decades discriminated against the Muslim minorities, for example, Sister Ann, a teacher at Anisa's school, blurts that Muslims should "remain at the bottom of the social hierarchy" (16) because they are an obstruction to the advancement of the church. Sa'id's decision to form an Islamic organization stems from this "unforeseen discrimination" to restore the purity of the minority culture and counter the influence of the essentialist majority group. Like Kabonyi in Ngugi's *The River Between*, Sa'id goes to the fundamental attributes like dressing in women to bring out those aspects that distinguish their culture from the dominant group's culture. For a marriage spouse, he says that he will not entertain girls like Anisa. He desires "a real woman properly attired when in public and not a plastic copy of a female" (85) like Anisa. Apart from restoring the ethnicity of the members of his association, Sa'id leads them to fight for the rights of Muslims at Rako Island to have their own school. They criticize the secular government by insisting that "the law that previously forbade the erection of Islamic schools must go" (267), the government fears a rebellion and gives in to their demands. Even when it offers to support the school, Sa'id, with his friends, rejects what they call *kaffir* assistance and declare that the school will only be financed by "rich Islamic states" (267). Furthermore, they reject foreign history and literature on the school syllabus and resolve that "the new syllabus is tailored to specific needs of the Muslim, offering education that meets the spiritual leanings and strengthens inherent belief in children" (268).

Islamic history and literature replaces the so called "*Kaffir* literature and history as it does not have direct bearing on the child's character development" (268). Arabic is taught as a second language to enable Muslims understand the holy book better. They demand total Islamization of the community's education because they find it tedious to pursue both secular and Islamic education. Sa'id's pursuits are quite essentializing in that they draw a line between the secular/Muslim which heightens the difference and subsequent polarity at Rako Island. The authorities become suspicious of Sa'id's revolutionary activities and he becomes a target of hostility. One day as Sa'id is trying to cross the street, a police car screeches to a stop and he is arrested, blindfolded and dragged into a car. The newspaper reports the arrest of two leaders of a drug ring in the Island. Sa'id and Usman appear in court over trumped charges.

The government is determined to stop Sa'id's activities since his appeal to ethnicity has polarized Rako Island. Whereas his personal secretary is not aware, the president has received complaints from influential people that are suspicious of Sa'id's separatist activities and feels threatened. They claim that he and Usman "are spreading ideas contrary to mainstream currents" (285) and their detention a deterrent to their incessant extremism. However, it heightens the tension at Rako Island as the Muslims threaten to rebel against the state.

Yusuf is a Muslim cleric in the United States and so is the embodiment of the Islamic norm in diaspora. As soon as Anisa informs him of her marriage to an atheist, Yusuf reminds her ideal Islamic traditions by sharing with her a scripture that condemns marriage to unbelievers, "[a]nd do not marry idolaters until they believe, and certainly a believing maid is better than an idolatress woman. Do not give believing women in marriage to idolaters," (142). He insists that Anisa should only read real Muslim scholars and reject all books written by non-Muslims. He advises that Anisa quits the marriage; however, having conceived Mike's child, she is reluctant. Henceforth, Anisa plunges in psychological problems as a result of the guilt she sustains from Yusuf's counseling session. He is so proud of his Islamic tradition that he denigrates that of the white majority. While interviewing Anisa about her marriage, he paints the West in dark colours and the East in light ones, for instance, he demands to know whether Mike commits the "western" vices: "[a]lso no drugs? No gambling record? No sympathy for nudists? No history of incest? No parental hate? No abortion advocating? No friend of Israel?" (138).

The "we/they" essentializing discourse is erected, where the Somali immigrants are upright and the Westerners, wicked. Such judgmental attitudes heighten tension and sour relationships between Yusuf and fellow radicals and the dominant white majority. He for instance draws Anisa away from assimilation who adopts separation and her marriage suffers constant friction. She introduces the Islamic traditions in the house, rejects her mother-in-law's gift of a puppy to her granddaughter, Nasra and denounces Christmas and Easter festivities. The narrator observes that it was "the whites, not Anisa, who did all the compromising" (171). Tension mounts between Anisa and the extended family leaving Mike's mother deeply aggrieved. She feels that Anisa has come to take over their life and dictate how they should live. She complains that Anisa has robbed Mike his identity by assigning him alien names. Charlotte, Mike's sister calls her a social misfit (170). She and her mother segregate Mike from their social circle; it is evident that cultural fixity adulterates both Yusuf's and Anisa's relationships.

Like Abdirahman in *Offspring of Paradise,* Yusuf has a place in the host nation's labour market. Nick Drydakis notes that "assimilation and integration dramatically increases the immigrant's wage whereas separation and marginalization decrease it" (393), owing to the tense relationship that the latter regimes erect with the dominant group. Amelie and Klaus reiterate Drydakis' assertion by observing that "labour force participation (by immigrants) is high when immigrants are integrated and assimilated and low when marginalized or separated" (12). Yusuf's obsession with ethnicity confines him at the Islamic Centre because his extremist views makes him unfit for any other job with the dominant majority. Anisa's life becomes unbearable after embracing cultural ethnicity; she cannot fit in her mixed marriage and is compelled to flee back to Rako Island.

4.3 Fixity and Hybridity, a Side by Side Comparison

This subsection looks at similarities between cultural fixity and cultural hybridity as strategies of resistance. In spite of their different manner of operation, the two strategies share a number of similarities.

First, they both are temporary modes that immigrant characters choose or leave depending on their goals in the immigration nation.

Singling out "separation, marginalization, integration and assimilation as measurements of ethnic identity", Epstein Gil and Odelie Heizler observe that "ethnic identity can change after the immigrants' arrival overseas" (15). The scholars mean that immigrant characters oscillate between the four measurements of self identity where separation refers to cultural fixity and integration, cultural hybridity.

In Abdi's novels, there are characters that at one point employ cultural fixity but abandon it later in favour of cultural hybridity. They vacillate between the two strategies of resistance. Anisa in *A Mighty Collision of Two Worlds* chooses hybridity when she reaches the United States of America. She likes western education and proceeds after high school to college in the immigration country. At college, she joins the company of white youth, who influence her by their leisure activities such as discos and parties to the extent that she stops praying saying that "she was too grown up for that sort of thing," (54). Furthermore, she falls in love with a white young man and sees him as persevering, "not pushy" (59) among a host of other virtues, the 'previous Anisa' would not have beheld. Nonetheless, after marriage, she denounces integration and adopts separation to resist the dominant group from inside. Mike, the husband, has to integrate by incorporating Islamic habits: "brush teeth before breakfast, use of water after toilet, use the left hand to take food, among many others to coexist with her. In *Offspring of Paradise,* Hana joins the company of the *carriers* and makes Helen her confidante, defending her against criticism by Muslim immigrants. She derides and mocks Usman, a symbol of the Somali brother whose sister cannot rely on. She asks him, "[w]here was your bravery when your brothers dumped me here in this cold?" (230). Her liking for the host community is so strong that she declares that she would never let a Somali immigrant know her mother's whereabouts yet the carriers, white people like Jason and Helen, know where she is. In the same vein, Hana scarcely talks to her Somali guardian, Mulki, but spends quality time with Helen, the white carrier. It is while Hana is with her at a ranch, *the Hunters,* that their relationship sours and Helen turns manic even threatening to kill her. The local police in the British town are aware of Hana- Helen friendship, which is why they arrest her as an accomplice in Rune's abduction. In spite of the friendship, which develops as a result of Hana's integration, she reverts to separation when Helen resorts to the use of force to convert her to Christianity. Hana attacks Helen's scorn at the unfortunate violence in African countries, reminding her of the Bosnian woman "raped and tortured by Christian Serbs" (271). Hana implies that political strife is not a preserve of African people as Helen wants to make her believe. Hana asks Helen why documentaries have not been produced to show the world the atrocities committed by the Christian Serbians. When Helen mourns about Hana having been her project for years, Hana, almost insolently retorts that it is not her "interest to be on anyone's list" (274). Their relationship goes to the doldrums because she uses cultural fixity to combat Helen's concealed cultural essentialism.

Secondly, both hybridity and fixity are essential in determining the identity of migrant characters. Cultural fixity assigns identities to migrant characters in league with traditional ethnic values of the ancestral land. Social scientists refer to it as ethnicity and characterise it with heavy reliance on "ancestral ties, kinship relations, common language, historical and imaginary memories and religious beliefs" (Gautam, 7). Stuart Hall describes cultural fixity as "traditional and shared" (393). Immigrants stick to the ways of the ancestral land and form isolated associations abroad. Gautam observes that the immigrants begin "formation of these associations "when friendly relations and interaction with host community become negligible" (4). The immigrant forms "a circle of friends" who he consults to find solutions to problems he faces in the foreign country. Anisa in Abdi's *A Mighty Collision of Two Worlds* starts consulting Yusuf and Khadija at the Islamic Center as soon she begins having problems in her marriage. Sa'id has formed an association or Islamic organization to ground themselves in ethnic values because Rako Island is a cosmopolitan society. Hana has a network of Somali friends: Usman, the fourth party that trails her, Abdirahman, her *Duksi* teacher, and Mulki, her reliable guardian who she turns to when their friendship with Helen comes to a bitter end.

Rainer Boubock and Thomas Faist refer to this as the concept of iconography, where diaspora preserve symbols of their culture, for example, "churches, mosques, synagogues, theatres, sports clubs, conference rooms, monuments and other elements that perpetuate memory of the motherland" (38). They observe that it is iconography that enables diaspora not to be diluted into the host society, and so maintain their distinct identity. In Abdi's works, there are characters that separate themselves to preserve their ethnicity, overseas. In *Offspring of Paradise,* Abdirahman rejects foreign culture at the refugee camp and sticks to the language and religion of his people. He starts a *Duksi* and teaches children such as Hana to memorize the Quran, which is both an attempt to build a firm foundation of ethnicity and an iconographical feature that perpetuates memory. The Quran is also a religious symbol that Abdirahman wants the children to retain to guard against dilution by the dominant group abroad. Furthermore, he makes a follow up to ensure that those children he has taught retain their Somali ethnicity. When Usman gives him a report about Hana keeping the company of a cunning white woman, he goes after her and finds her in what he considers an indecent hotel. He says "[b]ut I never thought I would find you in such a place [...] I am surprised to see you here, Hana. This is no place for you," (230).

Abdirahman's desire is to see Somali children grow up in undiluted ways of his people fashioned with untainted Islamic traditions. In *A Mighty Collision of Two Worlds,* Yusuf has established an Islamic Centre in the United States. With his wife Khadija, they have installed iconographical symbols of Somali culture, for example, Islamic library, a mosque and the Qurans. He discourages Somali girls from marrying non-Muslim white boys, to guard the Somali diaspora from dilution. While interrogating Anisa, his contemptuous attitude for the host community is revealed; for instance, he sees the whites as pro-zionists, and sex perverts: "No abortion advocating? No sympathy for nudists? No history of incest?" (138). He sums up by telling Anisa to terminate the marriage because Mike, the husband is an atheist.

Hybridity (as discussed in chapter three) is also crucial in construction of the identity of migrant characters. Hybrid identities are those that show strong attachment to both traditions of the country of origin and those of the immigration nation. As discussed in chapter three, these identities vary, for instance there is *shared sense* hybrid identities, where characters exhibit attachment to ethnic and foreign values in equal measure for instance Uncle Omar, Mike, Mohamed and Nasra in *A Mighty Collision of Two Worlds*. Furthermore, there is *in-between* hybrid identity in which characters oscillate from *ethnic skewed* identity to *Western skewed* identity. The characters are so unstable and assume identity according to the social context. The vacillation on the identity continuum results in trauma that causes the profound pain. Abdi depicts this via the characters Anisa, Hana and Hirsi in *A Mighty Collision of Two Worlds* and *Offspring of Paradise* respectively. Finally, there is the *ethnic skewed* hybrid identity where migrant characters embrace foreign cultures but more attachment to Somali traditions. The character Mulki, in *Offspring of Paradise* falls under this category. She works white community at the refugee camp as the English Somali interpreter and maintains cordial relationship with her white superiors; however, she rejects intimate relationships with the host community including love affairs and going to church. Mulki warns Hana against Helen's company and other extremities that might result in her assimilation.

Finally, both fixity and hybridity are immigrants' strategies of resistance against the culture of the dominant group. The character Sa'id in *A Mighty Collision of Two Worlds* is disappointed by the deliberate discrimination of the Muslim community at Rako Island and chooses cultural fixity to resist it. With his fellow Muslims, they criticize the secular government for denying them a school to learn Islamic traditions. They also attack secular literature and history, which they claim, does not make any significant "contribution on the children's character" (267). Tension mounts and scared of a Muslim rebellion, the government gives in to their demands, and even offers financial assistance. In the same novel, Anisa chooses hybridity to fight against the West by marrying Mike, a white man and converting him to Islam. She is then prepared to use the West to fight the West. When Mike's parents attack Anisa's beliefs, it is Mike who retorts, "[as] far as she is concerned, Allah is the God, and she is free to her beliefs. Everyone is free to her beliefs. Why are we denying her, her rights to her beliefs?" (174). Mike is the most suitable soldier in the battle against the West because she understands the rights and freedoms enshrined in the American constitution. When Anisa uses cultural hybridity she assimilates Mike completely till he relocates from the United States to Rako Island.

Cultural hybridity and cultural fixity therefore have similarities; they can be applied in isolation or concurrently to cope with alien cultures overseas. Characters select the option depending on their reasons for immigration, the gravity of the situation and their inherent dispositions.

4.4 Evaluation of Fixity and Hybridity as Strategies of Resistance

As observed in the previous section both fixity and hybridity are strategies of resistance at the migrant's disposal to cope with challenges overseas. In spite of the similitude, the two are not the same; therefore, this section analyses their merits and demerits and settles on the better strategy of resistance overseas.

Cultural fixity or separation is employed by immigrant characters in Abdi's fiction and the strategy has a number of merits. First, it enables immigrant characters to preserve their cultural heritage. In his study of on Indian diaspora, Gautam observes that "since ethnicity relies on ancestral ties, kinship relations, historical and imaginary memories […], it is a shield to protect and preserve ethnic culture" (7). In *Offspring of Paradise* the heroine, Hana, rejects absolute conversion to Christianity and any love affairs with the opposite sex with men in the dominant society. She avoids any tendencies that would usurp her Somali-Muslim heritage, for instance, when a white priest "dropped a round chip" (150), the sacrament, in her mouth, she spat it. The incident symbolizes her love for the Somali ethnicity and rejection of assimilation into the dominant Christian majority. The temptation to complete assimilation is enormous, for example, Helen offers her all the privileges to draw her into western Hellenism and materialism. She offers outings in posh cars, takes her to luxurious hotels, buys her sumptuous lunches and exposes her to Christian films and documentaries and even offers "to help her find a place of her own" (183) away from the refugee camp, farther from Somali immigrants. But Hana shifts her ground whenever her ethnicity and cultural heritage is threatened. Her grandmother's advice is a firm foundation of her cultural heritage. Dilapidated it may be, comprising destruction and anarchy, but she cherishes it, it is hers. In an internal monologue, the grand mother says: "wade and wobble through the mud, wade and rake up the dirt, and talk until there is nothing to tell. It is her life. Her painful life. Let her write. It is all she's got. It is her heritage, a fallen nation's legacy to her own; let the poor citizen record" (83). The grandmother refers to the painful history of Somalia, the history of political strife and destruction, which her grandchild, Hana should know and hand it down to posterity. Before Ayeyo's demise, she leaves a tape with Mulki containing all historical events from the assassination of Hana's father, Zahra's death and other tragic events to signify Gautam's "historical" attributes of ethnicity. Hana's choice of cultural fixity enables her to understand her cultural heritage and resist foreign influence.

For example, she reminds Helen *Ayeyo's* words when the latter tries to plant a wedge between Hana and Mulki. Citing Ayeyo's words, Hana replies that the Somali question is not bitter enmity but a simple case "of sibling rivalry" (143). Consequently, Hana forms relationships full aware that hers is a different identity. She keeps Helen's company, goes to school while performing Islamic rites like prayer. Rune observes that she has never abandoned her religion. He tells Helen, "[h]er religion is about the only thing she's got" (207), though she has lost all her close relatives, Hana has refused to let go those aspects of her ethnicity that define her. When white people attack her culture, she hits back in the same vein. She reminds Helen of atrocities committed by Christian Serbs against Muslims in Bosnia after she stigmatizes Africans as murderers. Hana's return to Mulki after her row with Helen symbolizes a final Return to her ethnic traditions and restoration of her "suspended identity" (Gautam, 7), almost untainted by foreign culture. Abdirahman, Hana's Quranic teacher, also retains his original ethnic identity. He teaches Somali children "Somali language and the Quran" (80) to perpetuate Somali cultural heritage abroad. He has started Muslim classes in the refugee camp for the same purpose. He inspires those betrayed by fellow Muslims by attributing their conflicts to God's trials. In spite of foreign influences, Abdirahman retains his identity in diaspora.

Cultural fixity paves way for compromise and change in the dominant group thereby laying the foundation of integration or cultural hybridity in the host nation. Those immigrant characters who stick to their ethnic morals compel the hosts to bend their principles. Gautam notes:

> Indian associations through their cultural shows, celebration of feasts and lectures have helped the Indian community in maintaining Indian diasporic identity. They have introduced the host society to Indian culture. The host culture has shown appreciation and supported the communities. The integration process has been a bridge between the Indian and host communities. (24)

Indian diaspora in the West stick to their ethnic traditions in spite of the constant discrimination. With time, the host community gets used to their presence and joins them to learn Indian attributes. Integration between the Indians and host communities is only possible when there is proper distinction between immigrant Indian community and the white dominant majority. Only cultural fixity or separation avails this distinction given its typical accentuation of "primordial and cultural differences" (Jenkins, 165). Integration entails merging of different cultures, which is impossible where there is overlapping of cultural identities. After marriage, Anisa in *A Mighty Collision of Two Worlds* reverts to cultural essentialism. She introduces Islamic traditions and denounces western traditions by condemning "Christmas, Easter and Halloween witchery and other festivities" (168). Mike's extended family reacts violently but it is through this that they learn they appreciate the difference between Muslims and Christians. Mike's mother learns that Muslims "consider the dog's saliva impure and when one comes in contact with it, they wash seven times" (179). In spite of the hostile reaction, Mike's white relations compromise and so Anisa manages to introduce Islamic culture to them. They keep dogs away from Mike's home and never arrange the parties in her presence.

Sa'id's Islamic organization rises against secular education at Rako Island. They demand the substitution of "British literature and history with Islamic ones" (268). The government is scared of their radical stance and gives in to their demands. They start a school for Muslims, which the government is even willing to finance. This is the same manner in which cultural fixity was applied in the fight for independence in Africa. Today, it is essential in the struggle for reform in many nations around the world through strikes, protests, and mass actions and sometimes, armed struggle, to put governments to task. One the other hand, cultural fixity has many demerits as a strategy of resistance against discrimination overseas. To begin with, it results in tension and violence between the two essentialist groups. The armed struggle for independence in many African nations pivoted around cultural essentialism or fixity to set stage for conflict.

Kwame Anthony Appiah observes that "for political purpose of acquiring independence after experiencing European colonialism, Pan-Africanists articulated themselves with their shared African ancestry to build their racial and political solidarity" (32). Pan-Africanists emphasized the beauty of African race and culture, a type of national pride that pitted African civilization against Western civilization in colonies hence a recipe for armed conflicts. In *A Mighty Collision of Two Worlds,* Sa'id emphasizes the beauty of Islam in all its purity. He becomes a Muslim activist who feels that assimilated Muslims at Rako Island are hypocrites; to him, atheists and Christians "are pagans" (266). The judgmental attitude he has underscores enmity between the two groups. Since non Muslims have dominated the Island for a long time, the Muslim minority seeks to subvert their authority. Sa'id's radical stance is viewed by the government as a threat to public security; subsequently, the state applies violence, Sa'id is charged with "framed charges of drug peddling" (267). Tension mounts to precarious heights. Had it not been the secretary's intervention, violence would have broken out. He accosts the president and expresses his fears that the two ethnic groups are heading for a "headlong confrontation" (286). Similarly, appeals to cultural fixity or ethnicity have a potential to destroy the family structure and the nation. It tatters the social fabric and annihilates the two institutions. Amelie and Klaus comment on the threat of cultural essentialism on the British social fabric:

The underlying motif of clashes (between immigrants and British hosts) is that the immigrant ethnic groups unite in identification to stand against the larger dominant society with which they share same territorial space but not same resources. (12)

This is the same scenario that is reflected in Abdi's *offspring of Paradise* where the minority clans like Mulki's form a militia group to unseat the dominant clan (Hana's clan) with "which they share space but not the resources". Claude Belanger observes that multicultural policies in Canada "have caused polarity resulting in social exclusion of ethnic groups and discriminatory practices that have affected their progress" (87). Somali clans that form the Somali nation embrace their own cultures and denounce other clans due to ethnic differences. Siad Barre's clan, the ruling clan, sees itself as superior hence denigrating the other clans. Siad Barre favours them with lucrative jobs no wonder Hana' "uncle is a high ranking official in government" (18). Ethnicity polarizes the nation: the ruling clan/ the other clans. Mulki's clan, the so called minority clans form a militia and the tension breaks out into open violence. Siad Barre is overthrown. Abdi writes:

> "[b]efore the general public grasped what was happening, this militia group had embarked on a wild rampage and blatant ethnic cleansing quickly developed into a full blown national disaster which inadvertently inflicted manifold misery as this nation of tribes plunged deeper and deeper into bloodbath and vandalism" (17).

Somalia is a typical reflection of the violence courting potential of separation or cultural fixity by elevating polarity. Innocent citizens from the ruling clan are branded *fagash,* loyalists and butchered. Hana's father is assassinated; mother escapes narrowly with a burnt eye and Hana escapes with the frail grandmother. Mulki's father tries to save Zahra but in vain. The militias are burrowing into the past to unearth the ethnicity of refugees:

>   Who is this?
>   Utiya…the great granddaughter of so and so
> So and so… who?
> The so and so who died and left behind only Utiya's grandfather
> So and so…remember that great uncle of ours? The one who married into so
> And so branch of the tribe. Which branch of tribe? (23)

After paying bribes to pass militia road blocks, Mulki's father decides to let Zahra hide somewhere and wait for the militia to clear away. The following day when they go to the hideout to get Zahra, they do not find her. Mulki's father feels that if his sons had agreed to protect Zahra at the hideout, she would have survived. An altercation begins and he reprimands his son, Abdullah, he assaults him. Abdullah has consistently killed members of the clan to which his mother belongs. Abdi writes, "[t]he same uncles who had loved them as their own were now on their nephews' execution list" (24). Abdullah retaliates and shoots his father. Mulki's family is been destroyed by cultural essentialism.

Another demerit of fixity is that it is retrogressive because the immigrant scoffs at new ways and refuses to learn progressive elements from the dominant group. He or she adores his traditions however parochial they may be. In Okot's *Song of Lawino* and *Song of Ocol,* the character Lawino rejects some progressive aspects of the West for its own sake. She says:

> I cannot use the primus stove
> I do not know how to light it,
> And when it gets blocked
> How can I prick it?
> The thing roars,
> Like a male lion,
> It frightens me!
> I really hate the charcoal stove
> Your hand is always charcoal dirty
> And anything you touch is blackened
> The electric fire kills people.
> They say it is lightning. (76-77)

The reader is left to wonder what is wrong with using the primus, the charcoal stove and the electric cooker as an African. The persona wants to stick to the use of firewood, which is a retrogressive way of thinking embraced by those who adopt cultural essentialism. Unlike Uncle Omar who views cosmopolitan environments as opportunities to learn, Sa'id in *A Mighty Collision of Two Worlds* goes to Europe for a number of years but refrains from music, dance and white women. He tells his fiancée, Faiza that he wants "a real woman, properly attired" but not modern women he describes as "plastic copy of females" (85). By so saying, he wants Muslim ladies to dress in traditional long dresses in spite of the advent of modernity, which stresses minimum body exposure among women for purposes of beauty. Sa'id Jibreel, the secretary's son, believes that the woman's role is to cook delicious food. It is a belief held by African Somali conservatives and so when he comes to woo Anisa, he attacks her poor cooking skills. He makes abrasive remarks about her cup of tea, which deals a blow to their relationship. Anisa is infuriated with him, wondering whether Jibreel is searching for a wife or a lady-cook. It is apparent that although cultural fixity has some merits, it is a recipe for violence among a host of other demerits.

Some immigrant characters opt for cultural hybridity in diaspora, on one hand; hybridity comes with demerits. Characters who oscillate between the culture of their country of origin and that of the host country sustain psychological problems. Bhabha refers to these identities as "in-between" identities, defined as identities in which humans are not "this or that" but are both "this or that" and neither "this and that". He stresses that hybridity is "a constant state of contestation and flux caused by differential systems [...] the unstable element of linkage" (227).

In *Offspring of Paradise* Hana's altercation with Helen and the latter's threats on her life after a long friendship disturbs her. Hana chooses integration with the white majority after her grandmother's death. He goes against Mulki's advice to meet Helen at school, in restaurants and church. She rejects her Somali circle of friends like Usman and Abdurahman and even dresses like white girls. But when Helen compels her to watch Christian movies and ethnically skewed documentaries, she turns to cultural fixity and defends her people against violence saying "Christian Serbs had tortured a Muslim Bosnian woman and pillaged her sense of hearing" (271). She feels low and then gets depressed after her narrow escape from Helen's claws. She consults a doctor and he diagnoses "a psychological disturbance" (342). Anisa, in *A Mighty Collision of Two Worlds,* chooses the middle ground when she arrives in the United States of America. She stops prayer, keeps white friends and assimilates by marrying a white man. After marriage, Anisa reverts to cultural fixity and suffers constant fits of depression. She recalls Yusuf's words from the Holy Quran that condemn "marriage to idolaters" and is overwhelmed by guilt (142). She regrets not having heeded Yusuf's advice to end the relationship. Even with a provident husband, good house and wealth, Anisa's mind is disturbed and is struck by insomnia. She cannot recite the *shahada* on account of guilt.

The constant oscillation between Somali ethnicity and Western culture is a harrowing experience that causes psychological pain in Anisa's life. Torn between a good marriage to a white atheist and a peaceful soul in her religion, Anisa reels in-between, worsening her unstable mind. Her psychological anguish stems from extreme worry about Mike's ability to raise the children according to the dictates of Islam. She enumerates Mike's imaginary weakness: he only prays when with Yusuf, he cannot fully accept her and that he hates Arabs. She denounces her hybrid status and refuses to forgive herself. In a few weeks of the identity split, she becomes a psychological wretch.

The doctor observes that her sickness stems from some sort of extremism and that is why he tells him to refrain from "religious bit" to start recovering (220). She is now unhinged, she shouts the *shahada* "for every jinni to think twice before messing her again" (222). Her ordeal depicts the flipside of in-between hybrid identities, once at the space, the immigrant suffers "abandonment neurosis" (Fanon, 144). In her self delusion, Anisa believes God has given "her perfect way of life but by consorting with the heathens of the world (like Mike) she had belittled herself" (223). She therefore denounces hybridity, replicating her guilt. Like Helen, she is proud, full of herself and suicidal. The doctor fears that she cannot be left alone, she might take her life. As she is discharged from the hospital, Anisa is schizophrenic. She hears voices: "[a]uthoritative voices fought for command over her, confronting her with conflicting messages and ordering her with irrational do's and don'ts. The narrator says that "Anisa felt like a Stone Age specter that had lived long ago and knew everything" (228). It is apparent that in-between hybridity identities are a recipe psychological trauma, which is devastating to the immigrants' personalities.

On the other hand, cultural hybridity or integration has numerous merits as a strategy of resistance. First, it has the potential to transform the immigrants or the host community into a new mutant. In *Offspring of Paradise,* Anisa assimilates the ways of the white community and is able and converts Mike into Islam. In three years, he learns basic Muslim laws and even bears children with her; forthwith, Mike cannot run away from the East. When Anisa flees to Rako Island, he is compelled to go to Rako Island to abduct the children. At the end of the story, Anisa confesses that by turning to cultural fixity, she had applied Christian strategies to convert Mike to Islam because "Islam does not allow for female clerics" (496). Indeed she had been educated and sent to the United States by the church. As a hybrid identity, she drops all claims to cultural superiority and says "she is no better than Mike" (494). The *carriers* also apply cultural hybridity to transform Muslim immigrants into carbon copies of themselves. Rune observes that sometimes they win "Somali immigrants on the spot" (206).

Furthermore, hybridity facilitates the exchange of ideas between the immigrant and the dominant majority. In her study of Kurdish immigrants in Sweden, Sulyman interviews Aram:

> I came to Sweden when I was twenty-two years and I have lived here for fifteen years. At the beginning, I felt I was still in my country (Iraq Kurdistan) but after five to six years, I integrated very successfully in the society. At that time, I had changed a little bit and found myself fifty percent each. I could not see myself as Swede or Kurd. However, after six years, I tried to change because the more one integrates in a society of another culture; the more one learns their habit from a particular perspective and cannot be part from it. But after a period of time, I did know that I am not Swedish in my face but some of their ideas have become part of my life. Therefore I can say that I have two identities, the first one is Kurdish and the second is Swedish. (28)

Aram has embraced many aspects of Swedish culture as he interacts with Swedish hosts as the latter get introduced to Kurdish culture. In India, "Indian associations through their cultural shows, celebration of feasts and lectures have helped the Indian community in maintaining diasporic identity and introduced the host society to Indian culture" (Gautam, 24). The host community, which is initially alarmed at Indianess gets used to them and joins them to learn their culture. Cultural essentialism precedes integration in a cosmopolitan community by facilitating exchange of ideas. The negotiation enables the two groups to learn a lot from each other to bolster tolerance and coexistence. When Anisa arrives at Fairwood, in the United States, she and Floor accommodate each other. Although Floor is initially astounded at what she sees as Anisa's "bizarre habits" (49), she becomes open minded and shares their diversity. Anisa had initially thought that Floor was insolent later but learns that it is just the

American in her; in fact "she is quite helpful to her" (41). Floor finds Anisa different, for example, she does not eat everything and her prayers make "her some sort of a freak" but Floor comes to accept "her friends bizarre habits" (49). In a dialogue, they exchange ideas about diversity in their cultures and discover differences between Rakon and American family structures. Mike and his parents exchange a lot of ideas about Islam and Christianity. Mike, for example, tells his parents that a "dog's saliva is impure" (179) in Islam and once a Muslim touches it; he should wash seven times. We learn that there is similarity between the Quran and the Bible when Mike's mother says that the Quran "is a copy of the holy Bible" (396). Mike retorts that there are many versions of the Bible and wonders which one has been plagiarized.

In her intimate relationship with the *carriers,* Hana learns a lot about them. She becomes as independent as Helen and Khadija's daughter, Khadra, envies her. She watches the *Jesus film* though reluctantly, and learns that Christians believe in salvation. Helen reads about Somalia and learns that there is rivalry among Somali clans, the knowledge of which she takes advantage to incite "Hana's loathing for Mulki" (183). She attends Abdirahman's classes to acquire knowledge on Islam ill intentions notwithstanding.

Hybridity results in peaceful coexistence. Albeit it is a strategy of resistance, its subtle nature of resistance maintains peace between immigrants and the dominant majority. To ward off clashes between the immigrants and host communities, the French government encourages cultural hybridity. Amelie and Klaus write:

> France's immigration policy has always been to integrate foreigners into the nation by putting into practice the

Enlightment and Republican assimilation model to efface ethnic and national origins in the second generation so that immigrant children can hardly be distinguished from French children. This model was strengthened by relatively relaxed citizenship laws and integrating institutions such as schools, military, unions and Catholic Church. It aimed at inculcating both French and immigrant children a common civic culture and pride of French values. (9)

The French government's objective is to reduce the native-immigrant interaction gap by encouraging immigrants to adopt native values. Once differences are reduced, the tense relationship between the two essentialist groups abates thereby leading to peaceful coexistence between them. In recent years, the French Supreme Court prohibited religious manifestations in public, for example, wearing the *chador* or Christian cross to discourage cultural essentialism (fixity) that magnifies the differences. In *A Mighty Collision of Two Worlds,* Anisa integrates in to the American society and gets a suitor there. The white community appreciates her and she is able to assimilate Mike from atheism to Islam without violence. No quarrel is observed until she adopts cultural essentialism by trying to impose her beliefs change on Mike and his white family. Uncle Omar warns her that if prophet Mohamed could not convince his uncles to become Muslims then no one "can force Islam on others" (314). Mulki coexists peacefully with the white community. She has learnt English and interprets for the refugee camp administrators, forging meaningful friendships with them. Her quick integration possibly owes to her strong educational background. Slobodan Djajic notes that "immigrants who arrive in their destination country with more human capital are thought to experience more rapid assimilation than those with fewer resources" (831-845). Her university education background enables her to acquire the English language fast enough to facilitate integration into the dominant white majority. Although she does not convert to Christianity, she coexists peacefully with "the white lady's tea party" (117).

Cultural hybridity bolsters the economic participation and stability of immigrants in the host nation. Alexander Danzer and Hulya Ulku observe that "a high degree of integration positively and significantly the immigrants income" (342). Immigrants who embrace the language and cultural aspects of the dominant group are easily absorbed in the host nations' labour market, for instance Mulki and Little Hirsi. The latter is so assimilated in the white society that he globe trots with *carriers* to spread Christianity. Like Mulki, he is the English-Somali interpreter, that has reaped a lot of material rewards from the *carriers*. They give him with his siblings the much needed material support. Hana appreciates them for what they do for Little Hirsi, supporting his whole family" (186). Later, he tells Hana that "the quicker the immigrant can pick the foreign captive's tongue, "the quicker you can cash your ransom money" (193). Hirsi's appeal to cultural hybridity has endeared him to the host community thereby bolstering his economic participation and stability.

Apparently, hybridity is a favourable strategy of resistance among immigrants living abroad. Cultural fixity befits the nationalist who are determined to fight for independence but unlike the nationalists who fights for freedom, immigrants are only but privileged by the majority to stay in the foreign country. It is therefore an act of wanton provocation for immigrants to apply cultural fixity as a strategy of resistance. The nationalists are in their nation and want to preserve the identity of the nation. Cultural fixity is apt for the liberation struggle;

nonetheless, Fanon warns that after the struggle, the leaders should now abandon it in favour of hybridity or risk remaining retrogressive. They will remain retrogressive because they will stick to their ethnic traditions and refuse to adopt the new changes that people are taking in league with modern science and technology.

4.5 Conclusion

This chapter set out by tracing the relapse of immigrant characters into fixity and analysed the change experienced in their relationships with the dominant group. It was interesting to note that relationships drastically changed from cordial to hostile with other ill consequences for example Anisa-Mike marital separation in *A Mighty Collision of Two Worlds* and a life threatening altercation between Hana and Helen in *Offspring of Paradise*. The second section analysed the relationships of fixed characters and the dominant group and found that all of them had hostile or tense relationships with the host majority. The next section compared hybridity and fixity and proved that they both are strategies of resistance. The chapter ended by evaluating fixity and hybridity as strategies of resistance. As much as cultural fixity is an effective strategy of resistance, it has far reaching consequences on the society including the destruction of the family and nation.

In *Offspring of Paradise,* in stance, Hana's mother country, Somalia, is almost annihilated by clans that set themselves against others because the pride in their culture degrades coexistence and the middle ground. Hana remains with her mother and grandmother as the only surviving kin, the rest annihilated. Cultural fixity replicates polarization of the Somali nation such that one's ethnicity becomes a license to live. The murder of Zahra is a case in point, where polarity is elevated at the expense of national unity. As a result, cultural fixity or essentialism destroys the Somali nation. These among many other demerits led us to the conclusion that cultural hybridity is better strategy of resistance given its bent towards preservation of peace. It eludes direct confrontation and shrewdly fights from inside the dominant group.

CHAPTER FIVE

5.0 Summary and Conclusions

5.1 Introduction

The study set out to examine identity politics and strategies of resistance staged by migrant characters in Safi Abdi's *A Mighty Collision of Two Worlds* (2002) and *Offspring of Paradise* (2004). The study argued that over the years, literary critics have explored the impact of postcolonial migration on identity negotiations of immigrants from Africa and Asia to western cities but postcolonial migrant literature from East Africa has received sparse critical attention. We therefore conducted an in-depth and critical analysis of postcolonial migration in the texts under study focusing on the strategies that immigrant characters employ to cope with discrimination by the dominant group abroad. The study also analysed the roles of migrant characters on themes typical of literature of migration and then interrogated Abdi's representation.

5.2 Research Findings

5.2.1 Chapter One
This chapter focused on the background to the study giving a detailed account of how the research was conducted. It laid the foundation of the study by reviewing ideas of migration scholars such as Robin Cohen, William Safran and Rainer Baubock. It then traced a historical background of Somali migration by reviewing historians like Robert Hess and Saadia Tooval. A statement of the problem showing the main focus of the study was then given as: this study examines identity

politics and acts of resistance staged by migrant characters living abroad. Using selected strands of postcolonial theory, the study investigates the role of hybridity in textualising migrant identity formation. The study then evaluates fixity and hybridity as modes of resistance. Finally, the characters are analysed to show how the two modes depict concerns typical of migration literature as a genre.

From the statement of the problem, the study derived three objectives that guided the study:
i) Discuss the role of characters on the central concerns of the novelist.
ii) Examine the role of hybridity in formation of diasporic identity.
iii) Compare and contrast fixity and hybridity as modes of resistance against the dominant group.

The study was then justified, that in spite of the efforts made by migrant authors in Somalia, they have received scant critical attention. This is particularly so among upcoming novelists like Safi Abdi, Nadifa Mohamed, Wavis Diriye and Abdirazack Osman. Most literary scholars in postcolonial migration have laid emphasis on migrant authors from Asia, Americas, Europe, Central and North Africa. The literature review on postcolonial migration and strategies of textual resistance was surveyed. Most of these scholarly works proved that the two strategies determined the identity of migrant characters. The literature review also confirmed that literature of migration has characteristic themes.

The postcolonial theory was outlined as the theoretical framework of the study singling out relevant concepts like orientalism by Edward Said, nationalism by Frantz Fanon, cultural identity by Stuart Hall, representation by Spivak and cultural hybridity by Homi Bhabha.

The study then outlined the narrative analysis qualitative design that was used to conduct the research. The research was purely library based and it aimed at achieving the main tenet of the design: viewing narratives as interpretive devices through which writers represent themselves and their worlds to themselves and others. The study sought primary data from two of Abdi's texts: *A Mighty Collision of Two Worlds* (2002), and *Offspring of Paradise* (2004). The study supplemented its primary data with secondary data from journals, books, dissertations, theses and projects obtained from the Post Modern Library and Literature Resource Centre of Kenyatta University. Online sources such as project MUSE and Sage Journals were also accessed at Post Modern Library. Data from primary and secondary sources was subjected to analysis to determine how Abdi textualizes her concerns at the level of characterization, how hybridity affects the identity of migrant characters and evaluate cultural hybridity and cultural fixity as strategies of resistance by migrant characters. Finally, the study pitted Abdi's concerns with themes typical of migration literature and then interrogated her representation to gauge its extent as a migrant author.

5.2.2 Chapter Two

The first objective of the study is explored in this chapter. Abdi's concerns are discussed, compared and contrasted with concerns typical of migration literature. It was discovered that most of themes such as hybridity, abandonment and return, identity and ambivalence are characteristic themes of migration literature. Abdis representation was subjected to Spivak's theoretical argument and it was found that the author misrepresented a large proportion of migrant characters.

5.2.3 Chapter Three

This chapter addressed the second objective of the study. It examined the role of hybridity in the formation of diasporic identity. It traced the steady transformation of migrant characters from cultural fixity to cultural hybridity when they reach abroad. It identified hybrid identities in the two texts and then analysed their relationships the dominant group. The study found that most characters vacillated between cultural fixity and hybridity upon arrival in western cities. Furthermore, many migrant characters adopted hybridity and affected the host communities to the extent of adopting hybridity too. Finally, the study found that most hybrid identities save for in-between hybrids who sometimes turned to fixity, had cordial relationships with the dominant white majority overseas.

5.2.4 Chapter Four
This chapter addresses the third objective. It was divided into four sections: the first section explored migrant characters that relapse into cultural fixity and how it affects their relationships. The study found that relationships shift from cordial to tense or rather hostile relationships when the characters abandon hybridity and choose fixity. The next section analysed the relationships between fixed identities and the dominant group. It was found that fixed characters had suspicious, tense and hostile relationships with their white hosts in the immigration nations. The third section compared cultural fixity and cultural hybridity as strategies of resistance. It was discovered that both determine the identity of migrant characters, both are temporary strategies that may be used in isolation or concurrently and both are effective strategies of fighting against discrimination. The fourth section evaluated cultural hybridity from cultural fixity by analyzing their pros and cons and it was found that although Cultural essentialism preserves ethnic traditions of immigrants, it is heightens tension and polarity between the immigrants and the host community

white cultural hybridity leads to peaceful coexistence between the two groups. The chapter settled on cultural hybridity as a better strategy of resistance by migrant characters.

5.3 Recommendations for Future Tasks

Migrancy is as old as humankind and literature is equal to the task to reflect the teething psychological and social problems that come with it. From the Jewish dispersal of 586 B.C, the forced shipment of Africans to Americas during Trans Atlantic Trade through to the *S.S Wind Rush* migrations after the Second World War, migrations have created a cosmopolitan society; consequently, the world should get enlightened about coping strategies to adapt to the culture of migrancy in our modern world. The present study, on coping strategies was conducted under the stated scope and limitation of Abdi's *A Mighty Collision of Two Worlds* (2002) and *Offspring of Paradise* (2004). The following areas can form new directions for further scholarship in relation to present day study:

Alienation as a coping strategy.

The study discovers that migrant authors and scholars emphasize cultural hybridity and cultural fixity as coping strategies in cosmopolitan cities and neglect alienation as a coping strategy. The study singles out some migrant characters that choose alienation albeit with negligible degrees of success to cope with discrimination of the host community.

Migrant Authors' Representation

While interrogating Abdi's representation, the study unearths many gaps in the capability of migrant authors to represent migrant characters abroad. After interrogating Abdi's representation basing on Spivak's ideas, the study discovers personal prejudices and contempt for a number of migrant characters. While speaking for fixed characters in *Offspring of Paradise,* she silences those characters that have chosen hybridity and alienation as their coping strategies. While speaking for hybrid characters in *A Mighty Collision of Two Worlds,* she silences fixed migrant characters. For Spivak, "the subaltern is heterogeneous" (79) and it is a hard task to speak for him/her. Nonetheless they cannot speak for themselves and so require the intellectual like Abdi to speak for them. After interrogating Abdi's representation as the migrant characters' voice, her weaknesses leave the reader questioning the eligibility migrant authors in their quest to represent migrant characters abroad.

Works Cited.

Abdi, Safi. *A Mighty Collision of Two Worlds*. Bloomington: Authorhouse, 2002.

—. *Offspring of Paradise*. Bloomington: Authorhouse, 2004.

Abdolali Vahdipour, Poujafari Fatemeh. "Migration Literature; a Theoretical Perspective." *The Dawn Journal* 3.1 (2014): 679-693.

Ahmed S. Castaneda C. Fortier A.M. and Sheller M. *Uprootings and Regroundings: Questions of Home and Migration*. New York. Berg, 2003.

Allermann, Antje. *States Against Migrants: Deportations in Germany and United States*. New York: Cambridge University Press, 2009.

Appiah, A. Kwame. *In my Father's House*. New York. Oxford UP, 1992.

Ashcroft Bill, Gareth Griffiths, Hellen Tiffin, eds. *Postcolonial Studies Reader*. London: Routledge, 1995.

Bahareh, Bahmanpour. "Female Subjects and Negotiating Identities in Jhumpa Lahiri's *Interpreter of Maladies*." 1.6 (2010): 43-51.

Bang, Anne. *Sufis and Scholars of the Sea- Family Networks in East Africa 1860-1925*. London: Routledge, 2003.

Battu Harminder, Zenou Yves. "Oppositional Identities and Employment for Ethnic Minorities: Evidence from England." *Economic Journal* 12 (2010): 52-71.

Baubock Rainer and Faist Thomas, eds. *Diaspora and Transnationalism: Concepts, Theories and Methods*. Amsterdam: Amsterdam UP, 2010.

Belanger, Claude. "Canadian Opinion of Immigrants: Pre-1945." *Documents of Canadian History*. Westmount, QC: Marianopolis College, 2006. 85-90.

Bhabha, Homi. "Cultural Diversity and Cultural Differences." *The Postcolonial Studies Reader.* Eds. Gareth Griffiths and Hellen Tiffin Bill Ashcroft. London: Rouitledge, 1995. 206-209.
—. "The Commitment to Theory". New Formations 5 (1988): 9-23.
—. *The Location of Culture.* London: Routledge, 1994.
Billing, Michael. *Arguing and Thinking: A Rhetorical Approach to Social Psychology.* Paris. Cambridge UP, 1989.
Bitek, P'Okot. *Song of Lawino and Song of Ocol.* East African Publishing House. 1972.
Bose, Sugata. *A Hundred Horizons the Indian Ocean in the Age of Global Empire.* Cambridge: Havard UP, 2006.
Bosma, Ulbe, ed. *Postcolonial Immigrants and Identity Formations in the Netherlands.* Amsterdam: Amsterdam UP, 2012.
Bozkurt, Idi. "Migration and Hybridity: Stereoscopic Vision in the Novels of Salman Rushdie, Mukherjee and Gosh". Windsor: University of Windsor, 2003.
Cairns, Stephen. *Drifting: Architecture and Migrancy.* London: Routledge, 2004.
Chiang, Chin Yun. "Diasporic Theorizing Paradigm on Cultural Identity." *Intercultural Communication Studies.* 19.1 (2010): 29-43.
Clarke, Simon. "Culture and Identity." *The SAGE Handbook of Cultural Analysis.* SAGE Publications 24 (2011): 506-511.
Cinnirella, Jaspal Rusi and Marco. "The Construction of Ethnic Identity: Insights from Identity Process Theory". *Ethnicities.* 12:5 (2011): 503-530.
Clifford, James. *Routes: Travel and Translation in the Late 20th Century.* Cambridge. Havard University Press, 1997.
Cohen, Robin. *Global Diasporas: an Introduction.* New York: Routledge, 2008.

Cooper, Rogers Brubaker and Frederic. "Beyond Identity: Theory and Society." 29:1 (2000): 1-47.

Danzer, Alexander, Ulku Hulya. "Integration, Social Networks and Economic Success of Immigrants: A Case Study of Turkish Community in Berlin." *Kyclos* 64 (2011): 342-365.

David Walters, Kelly Phythian and Paul Anisef. "The Ethnic Identity of Immigrants in Canada." *Joint Center of Excellence for Research on Immigration and Settlement* 50 (2006): 1-10.

Dirks, Nicholas B. Eley Geoff & Ortner, Sherry B. "Introduction" in N.B. Dirks, G. Eley and S.B Ortner (Eds) *Culture/ Power/ History: A reader in Contemporary Social Theory*. Princeton, New Jersey: Princeton UP, 1994.

Djajic, Slobodan. "Assimilation of Immigrants: Implications of Human Capital Accumulation of Second Generation." *Journal of Population Economics* 16 (2003): 831-845.

Drydakis, Nick. "Ethnic Identity and Immigrants Wages in Greece." *International Journal of Intercultural Relations* 36 (2012): 389-402.

Eliassi, Barzoo. *Contesting Swedish Identities in Sweden: Quest for Belonging among Middle Eastern Youth*. The United States: Palgrave Macmillan, 2013.

Elliot, Thomas. *Notes Towards Definition of Culture*. New York: Harcourt Brace, 1949.

Erick, Erikson. *Identity, Youth and Crisis*. NewYork: W.W.Nortons Company,1968.

Ericksen, Hylland. *Ethnicity and Nationalism: Anthropological Perspectives*. London. Pluto Press, 2002.

Fanon, Frantz. *Black Skin, White Masks*. Trans. Charles Lam Markmann. Pluto Press, 2008.

——. *The Wretched of the Earth, with Commentary by Jean Paul and Homi K. Bhabha*. Trans. Richard Philcox. New York: Groove Press, 1961.

Faulkner, Marie France. "Belonging- in- Difference: Negotiation of Identity in Anglophone Caribbean Literature". Anglian Ruskin University, 2013.

Finkelstein, Sydney. *Existentialism and Alienation in American Literature*. New York: International Publishers, 1965.

Fromm, Erich. *Sane Society*. London: Routledge and Kegan Paul, 1956.

Gautam, M. K. "India Diaspora: Ethnicity and Diasporic Identity." *Robert schuman centre for advanced studies* 29 (2013): 1-30.

Genetsch, Martin. "Difference and Identity in Contemporary Anglo-Canadian Fiction: M.G Vassanji, Neil Bisoondath, Rohinton Mistry". University of Trier, 2003.

Gregersen, Ida Aalstad. "An Interdisciplinary Project on the Post-colonial Novel Remembering Babylon". University of Troms, 2013.

Guenther Roth and Claus Wittich eds. *Max Weber: Economy and Society, an Outline of Interpretative Society*. New York: Bedminster Press, 1976.

Gundel, Joakim. *The Migration Development Nexus- Somalia Case Study*. Copenhagen: Blackwell Publishers, 2001.

Ha, Jin. *The Writer as a Migrant*. Chicago: University of Chicago Press, 2008.

Hall, Stuart. "Cultural Identity and Diaspora." Rutherford, Jonathan. *Identity, Culture, Difference*. London: Lawrence and Wishart, 1990.

Hardy, Thomas. *The Mayor of Casterbridge*. Backhampton: HarperCollins publishers, 1886.

Hess, Robert. *Italian Colonialism*. London: Chicago Press, 1966.

Hezler, Gil Epstein and Odelie. "Ethnic Identity: a Theoretical Framework." *IZA Journal of Migration* 4.9 (2015): 1-10.

Horney, Karen. *New Ways in Psychoanalysis.* New York. W.W. Norton, 1939.

——. *Our Inner Conflicts.* London: Routledge of Kegan Paul, 1946.

Holden, Anca-Elena Luca. "Cultural Identity in Contemporary German-Romanian Literature: Richard Wagner and Herta Muller". University of Georgia, 2010.

Huntington, Samuel. "The Clash of Civilizations." *Foreign Affairs* 72.3 (1993).

Hussain, Sabina. "Label and Literature: Borders and Spaces in in Postcolonial Migrant Literature in Australia." *Jasal* 3 (2004): 103-116.

Jackson II, Ronald. *The Negotiation of Cultural Identity: Perception of European Americans and African Americans.* United States of America: Praeger Publishers, 1999.

Jackominje Prins, Van Stekelnburge and Kalendermans, B. "Telling the Collective Story? Moroccan-Dutch Young Adults' Negotiation of Collective Identity through Story Telling: *Qualitative Sociology,* 36:1 (2013): 81-99.

Jameson, Fredric. *The Political Unconscious: Narrative as a Socially Symbolic Act.* Ithaca: Cornell UP, 1981.

Jean, Clandinin. *Handbook of Narrative Inquiry.* Alberta. Sage Publications, 2007.

Jenkins, Richard. *Rethinking Ethnicity: Arguments and Explorations.* London. Sage, 1997.

Jensen, Lotle. "The Dutch Against Napoleon: Resistance Literature and National Identity, 1806-1813." *Journal of Dutch Literature* 2.2 (2012): 5-26.

Krummel, Sharon. *Women's Movement: The Politics of Migration in Contemporary Women's Writing.* University of Sussex, 2004.

Lackland, Sam. "Psychological Acculturation of Young Visible Immigrants". *Migration World Magazine* 20 (1992): 21-24.
Lau, Esther Hor Ying. "The Migrant Experience, Identity Politics and Representations in Postcolonial London: Contemporary British Novels in Zadie Smith, Hanif Kureish and Monica Ali". Hong Kong: University of Hong Kong, 2008.
Luraschi, Moira. "Beyond Words: Mirroring Identities of Italian Postcolonial Women Writers." *Enquire* 3 (2009): 1-22.
Madut, Kon. "Ethnic Identity and Psychosocial Well being among New Canadian Migrants." *International Journal of Humanities and Social Sciences* 3.18 (2013): 85-89.
Malcom, Rebecca. "Spaces Between Identities of Transnational People Expressed through their Art and its Significance". Cairo: The American University in Cairo, 2011.
Mannur, Anita. *Culinary Fictions,Food in South Asian Diasporic Culture.* Philadelphia: Temple UP, 2010.
Mathew. "The New Testament". *The Holy Bible, Revised Standard Version.* New York: National Council of Churches of Christ, 1946.
May, Tim. *Qualitative Research in Action.* London. Sage publications Ltd, 2002.
McClosky, Herbert, John Schaar. "Psychological Dimensions of Anatomy": *American Sociological Review* 30: (1965): 14-40.
Meredith, Paul. "Hybridity in the Third Space: Rethinking Bi-cultural Politics in Aotearoa/New Zealand." *Te Oru Rangahau Maori Research and Development Conference.* University of Waikato, 1998. 1-4.
Meyda, Yegenoglu. *Colonial Fantansies: Towards Feminist Reading of Orientalism Cambridge cultural Social Studies.* Newyork: Cambridge Univeristy Press, 1998.

Meyer, Dagmar. "The Politics of Ambivalence: Towards a Conceptualization of Structural Ambivalence in Intergenerational Relations". *Gender Institute Networking Paper Series* 2 (2001): 1-10.

Mizutahi, Sitoshi. "Hybridity and History: A Critical Reflection on Homi K. Bhabha's Post-Historical Thought." *Zinbun* (2008): 1-19.

Mohamed, Nadifa. *Black Mamba Boy.* London: HarperCollins, 2010.

Montuori, Chad. "Gendering Migration from Africa to Spain: Literary Representaions of Masculinities and Femininities". University of Missouri, 2011.

Moslund, Sten. *Migration Literature and Hybridity.* London: Palgrave Macmillan, 2010.

Moudouma, Sydoine Moudouma. "Intra and Intercontinental Migrations and Diaspora in the Contemporary African Fiction". Stellenbosche University, 2013.

Mukundi, Paul Maina. "Preventing Things From Falling Further Apart: the Preservation of Cultural Identities in Postcolonial African, Indian and Caribbean Literatures". Ann Arbor: Morgan State University, 2009.

Odier, Charles. *Anxiety and Magic of Thinking.* New York. International UP,1956.

Olaussen, Maria. "Submerged History of the Indian Ocean in Admiring Silence." 56.1 (2013): 65-77.

Portes Alejandro and Rubiin Rumbaut. "Introduction: The Second Generation and Children of Immigrants Longitudinal Study": *Ethnic and Racial Studies,* 28:6 (2005): 983-999.

Quayson, Ato. *Calibrations: Readings for the Social.* London: University of Manisota Press, 2003.

Raj, Dhooleka S. *Where Are You From? Middle Class Migrants in the Modern World.* Berkely: University of California Press, 2003.

Rhys, Jean. *Wide Sargasso Sea.* Hermondsworth,1997.
Roland, Walter. "The Poetics and Politics at the Crossroads of Cultural Difference and Diversity." *Florianapolis* 48 (2005): 115-134.
Said, Edward. *Orientalism.* London: Penguin, 1977.
Saleem, Abdul. "Theme of Alienation in Modern Literature." *European Journal of English and Literature Studies* 2.3 (2014): 67-76.
Smith, Zadie. *White Teeth.* New York. Random House, 2000.
Spivak, Gayatri Chakravorty. "Can the Subaltern Speak?" *Marxism and Interpretation of Culture.* Eds. Carry Nelson and Lawrence Grossberg. London: Macmillan, 1988. 66-104.
Stets, Peter Burke and Jan. *Identity Theory.* Oxford. Oxford UP, 2009.
Sulyman, Areen. "Theories of Identity Formation among Immigrants: Examples of People with an Iraqi Kurdish Background in Sweden". Linkoping University, 2014.
Taylor, Charles. "The Politics of Recognition." *Multiculturalism: Examining the Politics of Recognition.* Ed. Amy Gutmann. Princeton: Princeton University Press, 1994.
Thiong'o Ngugi Wa. *A Grain of Wheat.* East African Educational Publishers, 1967.
——. *The River Between.* Nairobi: East African Educational Publishers, 1965.
Tooval, Saadia. *Somalia Nationalism.* Cambridge: Havard UP, 1963.
Tsolids, Georgina. "The Feminist Theorization of Identity and Difference and their Potential for Transformative Curriculum". Monash University, 1994. 1-22.
Wilde, Dieter De. *Neither Here nor There: The Immigrant Condition in Hanif Kureishi's the Buddha of Suburbia.* Ghent University, 2008.
William, Safran. "Diaspora in Modern Societies: Myths of Homeland and Return." *A Journal of Transnational Studies* 1.1 (1991): 83-99.

———. "Diaspora in Modern Societies: Myths of Homeland and Return." *A Journal of transnational studies*.1.1 (1991):83-99.
Wright, Richard. *Native Son*. New York. Penguin Books, 1972.
Virinder Kalva, Raminder Kahon and J. Hutynuk. *Diaspora and Identity*. London: Sage, 2005.
Young, Robert J. C. *Colonial Desire, Hybridity in Theory, Culture and Race*. London:
    Routledge, 1995.
———. *Postcolonialism: A very Short Introduction*. New York: Oxford UP, 2003.
Zimmermann, Amelie F. Constant and Klaus F. "Immigrants, Ethnic Identities and Nation State." *IZADP* (2012): 1-20.
———. "Work and Money: Payoffs by Ethnic Identity and Gender." *Res Labor Econ* 29 (2009): 3-
    30.
Zubida. H., Lavi L., Harper A. R, Nakash O. and Shoshan A. "Home and Away: Hybrid Perspective on Identity Formation in 1.5 and Second Generation Adolescent Immigrants in Israel." *Journal of Culture, Politics and Innovation*, 1:1 (2014): 2-4.
Zygmunt, Bauman. *Intimations of Postmodernity*. London: Routledge, 1992.

APPENDIX 1

Photo of Safi Abdi

Figure 1: Safi Abdi (www.youtube.com)

Figure 2: A Mighty Collision of Two Worlds

Figure 3: Offspring of Paradise

APPENDIX 2

Narrative Analysis

The study employed narrative analysis qualitative design. Tim May observes that narrative analysis "views narratives as interpretive devices through which people represent themselves and their worlds to themselves and others" (242). It focuses on the ways in which people make and use stories to interpret the world. It views narratives as social products that are produced by people in context of specific social, historical and cultural locations. May singles out four tenets of the design:

People produce accounts of themselves that are stored in form of stories

The social world is itself storied and people use stories to construct personal identities.

Narratives link the past to the present but:

There is no unbiased account of the past.

Abdi has therefore produced an account of herself in the two novels both as a Somali refugee in Dubai and economic immigrant in the United States. Through her novels, we learn the way Abdi interprets the world- a world of ambivalence, hybridity, cultural fixity or essentialism, identity crises and clash of cultures. Narrative analysis design seeks to understand human experience and social phenomena through the form and content of stories analysed as textual units. It uses field texts such as stories, journals, and interviews as units of analysis to understand the way people create meaning in their lives as narratives.

Narrative enquiry challenges the philosophy behind quantitative data gathering and questions the idea of objective data. Its emphasis is theorization of knowledge although it has been criticized for not being theoretical enough. Clandinin Jean notes that the focus of this design is "theorisation and organisation of human knowledge rather than collection and processing of data" (204). This implies that knowledge itself is considered valuable even when known by one person. Since it emphasizes themes (what is said) and structure (plot and characters), the design was pertinent in analysing the role of migrant characters on the concerns depicted.

APPENDIX 3

Tools for Data Analysis and Interpretation

The tools of data analysis and interpretation in this study were scholarly ideas on migration literature and the various strands of postcolonial criticism. The concepts of postcolonial theory included *hybridity* (Homi Bhabha, Stuart Hall, Frantz Fanon), *orientalism* (Edward Said), *abandonment neurosis* (Frantz Fanon), *identity* (Hall and Spivak) and *representation* (Gayatri Pivak). These postcolonial concepts were discussed in section 1.8: *Theoretical Framework*. Hybridity and fixity, for instance, were used to categorise migrant characters as hybrid and fixed respectively. Those migrant characters that demonstrated stability and consistence in their beliefs in western cities were named fixed characters and those that vacillated between foreign and mother cultures were labeled as hybrid. These hybrid and fixed characters were analysed to depict Abdi's themes such as polarity and political strife, cultural conflict, identity, abandonment and return, coping strategies (hybridity, cultural fixity and alienation) and ambivalence. The themes were compared and contrasted with characteristic themes of migration literature as established by scholars like Bhabha, Moslund, Abdolali and Pourjafari. The scholars established **ambivalence, coping strategies** (hybridity and fixity), **abandonment and return** and **identity** as themes typical of migration literature all of which are depicted in Abdi's novels.

Spivak's concept of *representation* played a vital role in gauging the accuracy of Abdi's representation of themes and characters as a migrant author. Spivak questions the notion of representation in postcolonial studies. She observes that poststructuralists crown the intellectual or the writer as a transparent medium through which the voices of the oppressed can be represented (67-72). Spivak contends that the colonized subaltern subject is irretrievably heterogeneous. She asks, "[c]an this difference be articulated? And if so by whom?" (79-80). In other words, to what extent does Abdi articulate issues of the **heterogeneous** Somali immigrants in western cities. The difference among the immigrants is so grave that the **transparent** medium (the writer) may find it very difficult to speak for all of them. There are those migrant characters like Abdurahman who adore their traditions and those who detest them. There are those in the third space. For Spivak, Abdi may either misrepresent them or in the attempt to give them voice start silencing others. An attempt to give the patriots (fixed characters) a voice will silence those who have assimilated (hybrid characters). Spivak gives the British example who in attempt to speak for oppressed widows by banning *Sati* rite (the rite of burying the widow with dead husband) ended up silencing the Hindu culture. Can Abdi avoid this act of silencing Somali culture while speaking for hybrid characters? Can she avoid silencing western culture while articulating issues of fixed characters? Even concerns such as hybridity, ambivalence, abandonment neurosis and identity do not affect all migrant characters in the two texts. Whereas some depict ambivalence, for instance, others are stable. Is representation of the subaltern plausible? Apparently, the subaltern cannot speak; therefore the intellectual (writer) is the sole medium that speaks for them hence making them susceptible to misrepresentation. The study applied Spivak's notion of representation to interrogate Abdi's works and discovered gaps in migrant authors' eligibility in their quest to speak for immigrants.

www.ingramcontent.com/pod-product-compliance
Lightning Source LLC
Chambersburg PA
CBHW010718300426
44114CB00024B/2894